32
33
34
35
40
67
69 101
70

Praise for *The Retargeting Playbook*

"Lauren, Greg, and Adam are THE experts in the field of digital marketing and retargeting. This books shows you why. With decades of combined knowledge and experience, there are few others who know as much about online advertising and the ad tech ecosystem. This new piece should sit on every digital marketer's bookshelf."

—Rachel Thornton
VP Global Demand Gen, Salesforce

"I LOVE this book. Do you like destroying your competition? Well, I do. And to do that it helps to have some sophisticated weaponry in your arsenal. Let them bring their pea shooter to the battle. I bring the big guns. If you enjoy topics like bottom funnel segmented nurturing via retargeting, then this book is for you. Or, if you just like to make more revenue, this book is for you. Lauren, Adam, and Greg are experts on the topic and give you the knowledge you need to dominate."

—Bill Macaitis
CMO, Zendesk

"How do you focus on 100 percent of your prospects? You get fantastic at identifying those that don't convert right away, and deliver timely and relevant ads that remind them of your value. Still don't know how? Let Lauren, Gregory, and Adam help you out with this excellent how-to guide!"

—Avinash Kaushik
Digital Evangelist, Google

"Anyone looking to grow a business should read this immediately. Retargeting is now an essential online channel and this book teaches you everything you need to know to run successful online campaigns. I highly recommend it!"

—Kraig Swensrud
Founder, GetFeedback

"*The Retargeting Playbook* teaches must-have marketing tactics—basics to advanced—for anyone doing business online. It's a comprehensive overview of retargeting from experts with authority, and should be required reading for any digital marketer."

—Jared Kopf
Entrepreneur, CEO and Angel

"For so many, digital marketing—let alone advertising and social media—is a deep, confusing pool of new terms and unfamiliar tactics. And so, I have to say . . . for anyone from Global Enterprise Digital Director to Small Business Owner wanting to understand how to harness the power of digital advertising, especially areas like retargeting, start with this book first!"

—Aaron Khalow
CEO, Online Marketing Institute

"It's about time someone wrote a book about this and explained how to get it done right. Lauren, Gregory, and Adam have done just that. Learn how to use this technology to woo potential customers back to your website and close the sale you would have otherwise missed."

—Mike Grehan
Group Publishing Director, Incisive Media

"As someone deeply passionate about earning traffic from inbound channels like SEO, social media, and content marketing, retargeting has proven itself to be an invaluable tactic to bolster the effectiveness of these efforts. But, it's a challenging undertaking to get started and even harder to optimize your efforts and achieve remarkable results. Thank goodness for *The Retargeting Playbook*, a superbly detailed—yet never overwhelming—guide to one of the most effective paid media tactics on the web. Lauren, Gregory, and Adam have distilled what must be thousands of hours of trial, failure, and learnings into a must-read resource for any professional in the web marketing field."

—Rand Fishkin
CEO, Moz

THE
RETARGETING
PLAYBOOK

THE
RETARGETING
PLAYBOOK

How to Turn Web-Window Shoppers into Customers

Adam Berke
Gregory Fulton
Lauren Vaccarello

WILEY

Published by John Wiley & Sons, Inc., Hoboken, New Jersey.
Published simultaneously in Canada.

For general information about our other products and services, please contact our Customer Care Department within the United States at (800) 762-2974, outside the United States at (317) 572-3993 or fax (317) 572-4002.

For general information about our other products and services, please contact our Customer Care Department within the United States at (800) 762-2974, outside the United States at (317) 572-3993 or fax (317) 572-4002.

Wiley publishes in a variety of print and electronic formats and by print-on-demand. Some material included with standard print versions of this book may not be included in e-books or in print-on-demand. If this book refers to media such as a CD or DVD that is not included in the version you purchased, you may download this material at http://booksupport.wiley.com. For more information about Wiley products, visit www.wiley.com.

Library of Congress Cataloging-in-Publication Data:

Berke, Adam.

The Retargeting Playbook: How to Turn Web-Window Shoppers into Customers/Adam Berke, Gregory Fulton, and Lauren Vaccarello.
    Includes index.
  ISBN: 978-1-118-83264-6 (cloth)
  ISBN: 978-1-118-88101-9 (ebk)
  ISBN: 978-1-118-88116-3 (ebk)
    1. Internet marketing.   2. Target marketing.   3. Customer relations.   I. Vaccarello, Lauren. II. Title.
  HF5415.1265
  658.8'72—dc23

                                                                        2013047047

Printed in the United States of America
10 9 8 7 6 5 4 3 2 1

This book is dedicated to marketers whose ideas
are bigger than their budgets.

Contents

Acknowledgments

ADAM BERKE

So "I" wrote a book. Not quite. This clearly never would have been possible without the support of the entire AdRoll team, who picked up the slack while we spent time discussing, writing, and assembling the content for this book. Particular thanks go to the Marketing and Creative teams, who all made direct contributions. I also need to thank my coauthors, Lauren and Greg. They contributed their unique and valuable knowledge, and without a solid amount of peer pressure, I'm not sure if we would have gotten this book done. Of course, I also need to thank my parents, Brian and Carole, who corrected my grammar, quizzed me on spelling (well, that part never stuck), and taught me to never be satisfied with a B+.

GREGORY FULTON

First off, I'd like to thank the marketers who have pushed the industry to innovate by demanding $5 for every $1 spent. Thanks to our customers for challenging us to come up with great solutions to their problems. Thanks to Aaron Bell for consistently finding new, interesting ways to keep me busy, and for encouraging us to write this book. Huge thanks to Stracka and Boodah for helping me keep my sanity while cranking through chapters. Most importantly, thanks to my mother for insisting that I love what I do and for never giving up on the dream that I'd be a writer.

LAUREN VACCARELLO

I'd like to thank everyone who made this happen, from coworkers to coauthors to customers. This is your book as much as it is mine. I'd also like to thank Rand and Geraldine for helping me take the leap to the startup world, and Kraig and Bill for their support and encouragement. Finally, I need to thank my friends for putting up with my constant absence and my family for both instilling confidence and keeping me grounded. I wouldn't be me without all of you.

CHAPTER 1

Why We're Writing This Book

Over the past three to five years, retargeting (or remarketing as it is sometimes called) has become a must-have marketing channel, alongside search-engine marketing and e-mail, for marketing to existing customers.

Retargeting has risen to this elite spot within the digital-marketing mix because it is a proven way to increase conversions and win customers who would otherwise be lost. When people look for products and services online, they seldom convert on their first visit. In fact, depending on the industry, 95 to 98 percent of people leave a website without taking the desired business action, such as make a purchase, fill out a lead form, download software, and so on.

Instead, people visit a site, then they check out competitors, they price compare, and sometimes they just get distracted. Retargeting allows you to stay in front of those people, who you know are interested in your product or service (why else did they visit your site?), and ensure they come back to close the deal.

However, despite the massive growth of retargeting adoption there is a notable lack of content around how the technology actually works, and little information about best practices for advertisers to take advantage of the channel. This is due to the fact that, historically, this type of technology was only available to large brands and agencies. Retargeting-technology vendors maintained high minimums since large amounts of manual work had to be done to execute campaigns. Despite the development of new solutions that make retargeting available to any size business, knowledge has remained locked up inside the technology vendors themselves, and perhaps a few savvy, performance-oriented ad agencies. Our goal is to unlock this information so that any marketer, whether you use self-service tools yourself or partner with an agency, can make more informed decisions about how to implement a best-in-class retargeting strategy.

WHAT IS RETARGETING AND WHY DOES IT WORK?

The common understanding of retargeting is that it is the practice of serving ads to people who have previously visited your site. However, there's more opportunity within retargeting than just showing people the same pair of shoes they just looked at on your site. To unlock these opportunities, it is important to first understand what makes retargeting effective.

To understand this, let's first look at what makes search-engine marketing so effective. Google is one of the great success stories of the Internet age, and much of that success is related to the fact that Google has a magic box that almost everyone in the world (except for maybe a few Microsoft employees) goes to and types in exactly what they want to buy, where they want to travel, and what kind of content they're interested in.

That type of data is called *intent data* and it is the most powerful data to use for ad targeting. It's the online equivalent of someone raising their hand and saying, "Hey, I'm interested in your product."

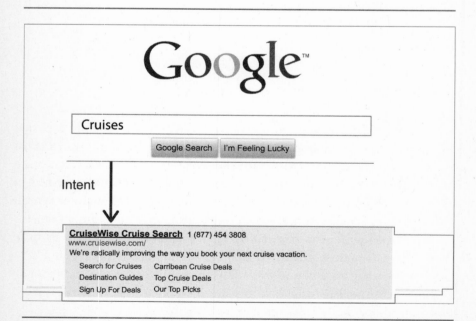

FIGURE 1.1 The Google Search Box Is a Key Way to See User Intent

When you run a search campaign on Google, essentially what you are doing is buying Google's intent data. Google is essentially a machine for capturing intent, and AdWords is an interface for selling it to advertisers.

Retargeting works so well (with performance similar to or better than search engine marketing) because it leverages the same intent data set. However, instead of someone typing something in a box that they're interested in, they express their intent by the behaviors they exhibit on your site. That might be visiting a product page, or by starting to fill out a lead form, or by putting something in their shopping cart.

However, people online seldom visit a site and immediately complete their purchase on their first visit, or submit their info, or whatever the business behind that site is hoping that they do. People shop around, they price compare, they look at competitors, and they just get distracted.

That's where retargeting comes in. With retargeting, marketers are able to tap into their intent data and target ads to very specific people who have raised their hands to say that they're interested in your product, but need to be followed up with before being won over as a customer.

FLAVORS OF RETARGETING

With the increased popularity of retargeting over the past few years, it has become common practice to relate other marketing tactics to retargeting. This can cause some confusion, as these tactics are all very different from the true retargeting (now sometimes referred to as *site retargeting*) we cover in this book. Examples include search retargeting, social retargeting, behavioral retargeting, and so on. It's almost as if there's no such thing as just targeting anymore, despite that being a more accurate term for many of these tactics. This misuse of the term *retargeting* can cause confusion as to what these other tactics actually are, what marketing objectives they solve, and what metrics should be used to gauge their performance. True retargeting (which is what this book is about) has sometimes come to be called *site retargeting* within the industry in order to clarify some of this confusion. However, to further clarify the issue, here's a summary of some other tactics that sometime use the retargeting moniker, but should not be confused with the type of retargeting covered in this book.

Search Retargeting

This tactic involves targeting people with display ads based on terms they search for across search engines and other web publishers where searches occur, such as comparison shopping sites. A more apt name might be *search targeting* since it is simply targeting people based on a particular characteristic. Similarly, we wouldn't call buying a TV commercial during the Super Bowl "sporting-event retargeting." This tactic appeals to marketers for some of the same reasons that retargeting does—search activity is a signal of intent. However, there are a few limitations to keep in mind when evaluating this channel. One is that scale for highly targeted keywords can be difficult to achieve. Since Google's move to SSL for all logged-in users, search referrer data from the largest search engine (+80 percent market share) is not available.

SSL is defined as secure sockets layer and is an Internet protocol that uses secure communications on the Internet. If enabled when logged into Google apps, Google will automatically convert you to https:// instead of http://. This does provide additional security, but when SSL is enabled and you are logged in when searching on Google, search referral data is lost.

Second, when users show intent by searching for something on Google, they are immediately interested in finding out more about a product and clicking on a link. This is not the case with search retargeting when they might see a display ad several days or weeks later while reading a site. For those reasons, it is best to think of search retargeting as more of an upper-funnel awareness channel. It allows for targeting users who have expressed interest in keywords relating to your product, but lacks the scale for highly specific terms, and does not reach users at the crucial moment that their intent is expressed.

Social Retargeting

With the emergence of paid advertising options across Facebook, Twitter, and LinkedIn, this term has become a catch-all for a range of tactics, making it particularly confusing. In practice this generally refers to targeting specific people based on their social actions. For example, targeting people who like your brand's Facebook page (fan retargeting) or targeting your Twitter followers. Some people have also referred to retargeting people on Facebook through Facebook Exchange (FBX) Social Retargeting. However, this would be more accurately described simply as retargeting people on social media inventory, if a distinction must really be made.

E-mail Retargeting

This one gets confusing because it is a term that is used to describe two unique things. Most commonly, it describes the tactic of e-mailing people who perform (or don't perform) a particular action on your site. Usually this involves sending people who abandon their shopping cart an e-mail about those items: a discount, a notification if they're selling out, and so on. However, sometimes people refer to *"e-mail* retargeting" as the act of placing a retargeting pixel in an e-mail to adjust their campaigns based on who does or doesn't open an e-mail. An example would be a daily-deal or flash-sale site that might not want to retarget people who open their e-mail because they already know they're reaching these people for free (aside from the cost of acquiring that e-mail address in the first place.) If people who read the e-mail don't click through, it can be assumed that they're not interested in the deal that day, so media spend shouldn't be wasted to further entice them. Alternatively, a brand might want to aggregate people into a retargeting segment who read their newsletter since they know these are highly engaged people. Either way, this is simply a targeting criterion and not truly e-mail retargeting as described above.

To address the proliferation of the word *retargeting*, the typical form of retargeting we cover in this book is referred to as *site retargeting*. This clarifies that the marketer is targeting people who have previously browsed their website.

UNDERSTANDING THE CUSTOMER JOURNEY

As a marketer or business owner, you probably spend a lot of time thinking about the customer journey and what you can do to influence it. In the most classic form, the buyer becomes aware of your product or service, moves through the consideration cycle, and then makes the purchase. The customer journey is evolving even further and now has to account for peer-to-peer influence through social networks and needs to more strongly consider customer lifetime value.

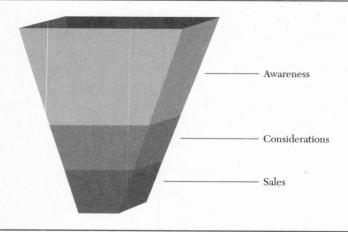

Awareness

Considerations

Sales

FIGURE 1.2   The Top of the Sales Funnel Is Defined as the Awareness Phase, the Middle as the Consideration Phase, Which Leads to Purchase.

Depending on your business and cost of sale, this customer journey can take a few moments, like in the case of some low-cost items purchased online, or a few years for multimillion-dollar, business-to-business (B2B) purchases. Let's face it, with an increasing number of devices and the speed of technology your prospects are more likely to get distracted throughout every phase of the process. Research is no longer about reading a few industry reports and making a decision—now it involves crowdsourcing information on social networks, like Facebook. During the consideration phases, your prospects are quickly price comparing while you are figuring out new ways to differentiate your product or services. Sales aren't guaranteed as the funnel has leaked the majority of your prospects as they made the journey through the buying process. Shopping cart abandonment rates vary from 50 to 70 percent as buyers are decide to buy a product elsewhere or just get distracted by everyday life. Closing that sale, whether it is in B2B or B2C, has gotten more difficult and will continue to do so if marketing tactics don't evolve as the consumer does.

Providing consumers with tailored experiences where both content and advertising is personalized to their needs and interests increases relevancy and, ultimately, long-term sales. Throughout the course of this book, we will give you practical tips on how you can use retargeting to increase awareness among your consumer base. We will also share how to use retargeting to drive sales and help bring back cart-and-form abandoners, as well as discuss how retargeting can be used to nurture leads through the sales cycle. As the customer journey is changing, we will also discuss how to use FBX to communicate with your customers and prospects. Over the course of this book, we will also cover how to look beyond the first sale and think about how retargeting can help increase customer lifetime value and build community.

TYPICAL STATS AND ROI

Forrester Research reports that on average only 3 percent of shoppers make a purchase during their first visit to an online store. Of the remaining 97 percent, 71 percent place an item in their shopping cart but end up abandoning it. So what are the top reasons they're hesitant to buy?

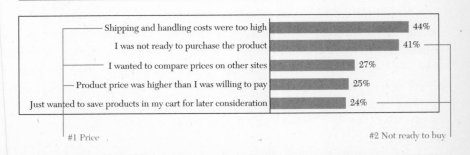

FIGURE 1.3   Reasons Why People Abandon Carts

Retargeting is a great way to re-engage with those cart abandon-ers and get them back to your website. What type of results can you expect with your retargeting programs? That is going to vary by indus-try and by your goals, but we want to give you some ideas of where to start. AdRoll ran a customer survey and asked 2,000 participants to compare performance of their retargeting campaigns with their search program. Sixty-two percent of respondents said that retarget-ing performs as well as or better than search. Participants were also asked to compare performance of their retargeting programs with the rest of their display programs. Eighty-nine percent of respondents said that retargeting performs as well as or better than other forms of display.

When trying to determine how to use metrics in your retargeting program, it is best to start by looking at performance of current market-ing initiatives. For example, if you are going to use retargeting to drive free trial sign-ups, and your search program has the same goals, start by looking at your average cost per sign-up for search. Now, also look at all other forms of online advertising that have the same goal, like traditional display, social, or lead buys. Retargeting performance should be com-pared with these similar programs.

We have a customer in the financial vertical who has a $40 cost per sign-up with search, and a $7 cost per sign-up with retargeting. Although such a big gap isn't typical, it is possible for retargeting to outperform search programs, especially in verticals where paid search cost per clicks are quite high. With that in mind, we aren't recommend-ing turning off your search programs, but instead looking at the holistic online marketing environment and investing accordingly.

Your retargeting click-through rate (CTR) is also going to vary based on your ads. In Chapter 6, we discuss several best practices to help improve CTRs like clear calls to action and the use of product imag-ery and model imagery depending on placement. For advertisers in the retail vertical, we've found that LiquidAds, or dynamic, personalized creative ads, have a significant impact on performance. For example, a leading menswear company, Indochino, saw a 102 percent increase in CTRs with dynamic product ads versus the use of static ads.

A Quick Lesson in Retargeting Terminology

Throughout the course of this book, we will call out and define industry-specific terminology, but we want to make sure everyone has a solid understanding of a few key terms before diving into the rest of the book.

- CPM: Literally translated as *cost per mille*, CPM is the most common form of pricing online advertising. Advertisers are charged a price per thousand impressions served.
- CPC: Another common form of pricing in the online advertising world is CPC or cost per click. Advertisers are charged when ads are clicked on.
- CPA: Defined as cost per acquisition. Advertisers are charged when an agreed-upon acquisition action is achieved.
- LiquidAds: This is a form of dynamic, personalized advertising. For example, when a website visitor views a particular product and then browses the web, the product view or a suggested product appears in the advertising.
- Intent signals: This is something that the potential customer does that signals "I'm interested in this product or service." It could be a specific page visited, like a product page, or an action taken, such as items placed in a cart.

LET'S GET ROLLING!

Now that you have the basics down, it's time for the fun part. Over the course of this book we will walk you through everything from setting up your retargeting campaign, best practices, and case studies to advanced strategies, and how the world of real-time bidding has revolutionized the industry and ultimately drives ROI. We hope you enjoy reading this as much as we enjoyed writing it.

CHAPTER 2

The Evolution of Display Advertising

In 2012 the online advertising spend exceeded $100 billion for the first time ever, with 48 billion of those dollars going to display ads.[1] Performance display is becoming an increasingly hot topic, with billions of those dollars going to interactive ad units that are geared to increase both brand awareness and engagement. How did an ad product that originated in the mid-1990s to help build brands via direct-publisher buys become a technologically infused powerhouse that drives measurable results for hundreds of thousands of businesses? Let's find out.

HOW DISPLAY WORKS

Online ads are purchased by an advertiser (anyone who wants to run online ads) from a publisher (any website that serves online ads). Primarily, this is done by purchasing a quantity of ad impressions (an ad impression is simply defined as an ad displaying on a web site) for a price-per-1,000 ad impressions. We'll speak at length about the various ways that these buyers and sellers come together in this chapter.

HISTORY OF DISPLAY

Before we dive into how the display landscape functions today, let's take a step back in time to better understand how it got where it is today. When the Internet hit its awkward preteen stage in the mid-1990s,

---

[1]http://www.emarketer.com/Article/Digital-Account-One-Five-Ad-Dollars/10095 92#7RipU565WFH7DvTv.99.

website owners started to realize that they could make a great deal of money by selling ads on their sites. At the time, that meant that each website had a salesperson contact potential advertisers and offer to sell them a quantity of ad impressions at a negotiated price.

For the most part, this model was operating under a strategy referred to as *contextual targeting*. Contextual targeting is the practice of showing ads on a website because the content on that site is contextually relevant to the group of customers you are trying to reach. For example, if you are selling golf balls, you would run ads on golf-specific web sites. But you also might run ads on financial websites, as financial professionals are often golf enthusiasts. Additionally, you might run ads on a site about high-end sports cars, as golfers tend to be high-net-worth individuals. Contextual targeting relies on the assumption that if a site visitor is interested in content about a specific topic, then they are also probably interested in a given advertiser's specific products or services.

This led to large websites hiring direct sales teams. These teams would reach out to potential advertisers whose products or services were aligned with the content of their site. Many of these advertisers were looking to drive brand awareness, referred to as *brand advertising*. However, in the early stages of the Internet, something interesting happened that led to the explosion of *direct response marketing*. Direct response is online advertising designed to drive a very specific action, such as signing up for a newsletter, filling out a lead generation form, or actually purchasing a product or service online.

The Internet lent itself incredibly well to direct response marketing due to the simple fact that Internet marketing is incredibly measurable. Prior to online marketing, it was very difficult to attribute a sale to a specific marketing initiative. For years, the advertising industry did countless studies and poured millions of dollars into proving that their campaigns were having an impact, and they were able to prove the overall impact of a campaign to a degree. Then a new, highly measurable channel emerged, and marketing dollars began to shift to the web.

Direct response advertising led to a newfound value in online advertising. However, it is also what gave online advertising a bad reputation in the early days. The famous dancing aliens ads, pop-up ads, advertising cheap mortgage rates, and a slew of other spammy ads were prevalent, and appeared to dominate the landscape simply because they were the most eye-catching.

FIGURE 2.1   The Infamous Dancing Alien Mortgage Ad

However, as marketers and website browsers both became more sophisticated, online advertising was forced to mature. Dancing alien ads gave way to highly relevant ad units targeted to a specific individual, but we'll cover that shortly.

THE EMERGENCE OF AD EXCHANGES

Earlier in this chapter, we touched upon the first way in which buyers and sellers of online ads came together: the direct sales approach. This evolved into the ad-network model. An ad network connects advertisers with websites that want to sell ad impressions. In this new model, an ad network would aggregate multiple sites into a marketplace, often (but not always) around a given industry vertical, such as fashion or travel, and then sell a predetermined number of ad impressions on those sites to advertisers for a contracted amount. Now, rather than buying advertising on a single site in a one-to-one relationship, advertisers were able to purchase ads across a number of sites that they felt their potential customers were likely to frequent.

In the early days, there were two main types of ad networks: vertical and blind. Vertical ad networks were typically transparent in that they revealed to the advertiser exactly which sites would run their ads. Blind ad networks, however, were not transparent. While often cheaper, blind networks wouldn't reveal to the advertiser exactly where ads were running. So while advertisers were now able to buy online advertising in larger quantities across a variety of sites in a more streamlined fashion, the model still lacked sophistication.

In April 2007 a major change took place in the industry. Yahoo! acquired the Right Media Exchange (RMX), and Google purchased DoubleClick. These two new platforms created what we refer to as an *ad exchange*. An ad exchange is huge marketplace made up of many ad networks, individual websites, and large publishers. It is a technology platform that facilitates the bidding for buying and selling of online advertising. These two large exchanges, now backed by two of the largest companies in Silicon Valley, consolidated the majority of the web into two access points. A few other ad exchanges quickly emerged, and this competition began to drive innovation in the online advertising industry.

Many of the website publishers whose ad inventory was previously only available through direct relationships with publishers or ad networks was now made available through a few ad exchanges. Essentially, a buyer could now reach the entire Internet through just a handful of partners, rather than having to maintain relationships with hundreds of websites individually. After this shift, it became necessary to rethink how online advertising was being purchased. Prenegotiating the price of impressions works for a single website, or even on a group of websites. However, how do you determine the value of ad impressions when you have access to the entire Internet?

To simplify the evolution of the display advertising ecosystem, let's pretend we are shopping for a new wardrobe. The original model where websites sold their ad inventory directly to brands would be like shopping at each designer store individually. You would need to go directly to the Tommy Hilfiger store for some pants, then go to the Polo store for a shirt. The ad-network model would be like going to a department store, where you could walk into the menswear section and shop certain brands under one roof. The ad-exchange model would be like a large shopping mall that contained all of the major department stores, many small boutiques, and all of the designer shops. And while navigating such a mall in the real world sounds daunting, the advent of programmatic buying, or real-time bidding, made the online advertising version of this not only manageable, but incredibly powerful.

REAL-TIME BIDDING EXPLAINED

The most impactful change driven by the emergence of these ad exchanges has been the birth of what we refer to as real-time bidding (RTB). Bringing all of the online advertising inventory under one roof provided a newfound flexibility in how we are able to value, and therefore purchase, ads across the web.

Prior to RTB, a buyer and seller would negotiate a set price for a set amount of ad impressions up front. The buyer may have been a brand, or an agency representing that brand. The seller was either the sales team representing a website publisher or an ad network representing a number of sites.

In this model, a typical use case is as follows:

Brand X sells men's outdoor apparel. Their target audience is men, ages 18 to 34, who are active, athletic, and make enough money that they can pay up for high-quality outerwear.

Brand X contacts sportsite.com, and negotiates a deal to serve their ads on that site. They set a budget of $20,000. Sportsite.com is willing to serve those ads for a price of $10 per 1,000 ads shown. This pricing is called a *CPM*, or cost per mille (mille is the Latin word for 1,000)—it is the most common way for online advertising to be sold.

In this case, Brand X knows that they will show their ads 2,000,000 times for $20,000 dollars. Every impression is priced exactly the same. So regardless of whether this is the first, fifth, or tenth time a user has seen an ad, it costs the same. However, as marketers, we know that not every website visitor is created equal.

On the other hand, RTB allows advertisers to evaluate a single impression at the time it is rendering, determine its value, and then bid in an open auction for the right to serve an ad. It also allows you to take into account everything that you may know about a given Internet user to determine how valuable that user is for your brand. This is a significantly more efficient way to shop, as you're not locked into a price in advance. You'll only pay one cent more than the next highest bidder is willing to pay for the same ad impression. As with all fair markets, competition breeds the fairest price, and online advertising is no different.

Let's go back to the above example, but let's employ RTB. To do so, we'll need to include some new players in this game. Sportsite.com, in order to be accessible via RTB, must be working with one of the major *ad exchanges*, like Google's DoubleClick, which was rebranded AdX. Brand *X* must be buying through an RTB-enabled buyer. Let's call them AdRTB.

An Internet user visits sportsite.com. AdX, the ad exchange that is integrated with sportsite.com, makes a server call to AdRTB and says, "AdRTB, are you interested in serving an ad to this user on sportsite. com?" AdRTB has milliseconds to decide whether they want to serve an ad to this user. They will do so based on a number of data points that vary based on the provider, advertisers, and campaign. If they value this impression, they determine how much that ad impression is worth to them, and then return a bid to the auction as well as the ad that they want to show. If their bid is the highest, then Brand *X* shows the ad on sportsite.com. This all happens in the amount of time it takes for a web page to render, typically less than 100 milliseconds.

Armed with these sophisticated buying engines, marketers were no longer content to select a list of websites and purchase advertising across them. Marketers shifted their focus to wanting to reach specific web users. This trend, coupled with ad exchanges and RTB, gave birth to a new breed of advertising-technology companies. These new companies, made up of retargeters, demand-side platforms (DSPs), and data-management platforms (DMPs), were all created in order to drive incredibly intelligent purchasing of online advertisements. Staffed with data scientists, rocket scientists, and PhDs, these companies put a tremendous amount of energy into developing the algorithms that determine the value of a given ad impression. This newfound sophistication was brought on by the next big shift in online advertising: the emergence of cookie-based targeting.

COOKIES

A *cookie*, also referred to as an *http cookie* or *web cookie*, is a small amount of data sent from a website and stored in the web browser on a computer. This has many uses. Ever wonder why when you go back to Facebook it remembers who you are and keeps you logged in? That's because Facebook keeps track of your logged-in state in a cookie.

```
<script type="text/javascript">
adroll_adv_id = "NJKMB4KMGJGJDLM2LNPOL3";
adroll_pix_id = "GUIAXC4EBZECDBYY6ENT2M";
(function () {
var oldonload = window.onload;
window.onload = function(){
   __adroll_loaded=true;
   var scr = document.createElement("script");
   var host = (("https:" == document.location.protocol) ? "https://s.adroll.com" :
"http://a.adroll.com");
   scr.setAttribute('async', 'true');
   scr.type = "text/javascript";
   scr.src = host + "/j/roundtrip.js";
   ((document.getElementsByTagName('head') || [null])[0] ||
    document.getElementsByTagName('script')[0].parentNode).appendChild(scr);
   if(oldonload){oldonload()}};
}());
</script>
```

FIGURE 2.2   Snippet of JavaScript Representing a Web Cookie

Another use for cookies is site analytics. An e-commerce shop will use them to keep track of onsite behaviors in order to optimize the experience for their customers. They are used for conversion tracking, A/B testing, and numerous other components of online marketing. For online advertising, cookies are a technology that can be used to understand the intent or interests of a user. When a potential customer visits BrandX .com, a cookie may be placed in that customer's browser. Brand *X* may then store in the cookie the pages that customer visits, what products they look at, and whether or not they purchased something. That information allows Brand *X* to market to the people who have taken actions that they deem to be intent signals. We'll talk about how to leverage this information later.

The important thing to know about cookies is that they are anonymous and the user can delete them at any time. Brand *X* doesn't know the name of the customer browsing their site. They do not know the e-mail address unless the customer has provided it to them. All that they know is that a particular web browser has taken certain actions on their site. An anonymous ID, such as cookie12345, will be assigned to that browser so that it may be distinguished from other browsers. But the information collected is not personally identifiable information (PII).

So how do the sophisticated buying engines that we described previously use cookies to assign a value to an ad impression in real time and run highly targeted advertising? It all starts with ad technology companies placing their *tags* throughout the web. A tag is a small snippet of code, or a very small imperceptible image, that allows ad-tech companies to drop the previously described cookies into a web browser.

THE REAL-TIME ADVANTAGE

The most powerful display-advertising technique unlocked by RTB is, without a doubt, retargeting. Retargeting allows marketers to continue the dialog with their potential customers after they've left the store. Because RTB allows you to value each ad impression on the web independently, it also allows you to decide what is an important signal to you as a marketer, and then assign values to those signals to be used while bidding.

Would you pay the same for the right to show an ad to someone who bounced off of your homepage three weeks ago compared to someone who abandoned your shopping cart five minutes ago? Would you value someone who browsed a $10 pair of socks on your e-commerce site equally to someone who checked to see if a $500 dress was available in her size? Would you value an impression on the homepage of nytimes.com the same as one buried at the bottom of your best friend's cooking blog? RTB allows you to value those different customers and impressions based on everything that you know about them. It ensures that your ad spend is directed towards the customers who are going to drive the most value for your business. While this may sound complicated and daunting, with the right retargeting partner, sophisticated marketing like this is as easy as sending an e-mail blast.

Let's say that you're the marketing manager at arfscarfs.com, an online boutique specializing in scarfs for dogs. You have a retargeting tag on your site that can capture intent data about your customers as they browse dog scarfs on your site. Let's say Lauren, a dog-scarf enthusiast, is shopping on arfscarfs.com. She puts three dog scarfs into her shopping cart. But, as dog-scarf enthusiasts often do, she gets distracted and leaves without completing the purchase. Obviously she is someone who is very close to making a purchase; she just needs to be reminded or maybe nudged a bit.

What retargeting with RTB allows you to do is this: When Lauren is checking out Dwell.com or browsing Facebook, a signal is sent back that says, "Hey, cookie id12345 is on the Internet . . . how much is that worth to you?" Within 100 milliseconds an RTB company will evaluate a number of factors to determine how valuable it is for a given advertiser to serve an ad to a particular user and then return a bid for that amount. For arfscarfs.com, serving an ad to Lauren on Facebook might be worth a $4 CPM. That bid would enter the auction, and if it was the highest bid, arfscarfs.com would serve Lauren an ad to bring her back to convert. Lauren makes the purchase, arfscarfs.com makes a sale, and Lauren's dog gets a new scarf. It's win-win-win.

It's called real-time bidding, but what makes it powerful is that it's real-time decision making. RTB allows you to make informed decisions about every impression that you buy on the Internet. It allows you to serve the right message to the right potential customer at the ideal time. If your retargeting partners don't have their own RTB technology, then you are not getting the full value of retargeting.

CHAPTER 3

Getting Started

Who Should Use Retargeting and for What

Retargeting has emerged as the premiere online advertising tactic, but how do you know if it is right for you and when to use it? This chapter will walk you through choosing a retargeting platform, setting up your first retargeting campaign, and selling retargeting internally, because your budget needs to come from somewhere.

YOU HAVE A WEBSITE, NOW WHAT?

Congratulations, you have a great website and visitors are converting, but are all visitors buying your product? Chances are, probably not. In fact, 98 percent of website visitors leave without filling out a form or purchasing anything. That is where retargeting comes in. Retargeting allows you to message the 98 percent of people who don't buy and ultimately bring them back to your website.

To get started with retargeting, you must have your own website. Unfortunately, if you only have a Facebook page, retargeting will not work for you at this time. You also need visitors coming to your website. If you have a website with at least 5,000 monthly unique visitors, then retargeting may be a great option for you to increase your brand awareness and drive incremental sales.

HOW TO CHOOSE A RETARGETING PLATFORM

Congratulations—you are ready to get started with retargeting. Now it is time to choose which retargeting platform is right for your business. There are a lot of different options out there so this part can be a bit daunting. Below are some things you should consider when deciding which retargeting platform to go with.

- *Reputation*. What is the retargeting platform you are going with known for and does it align with your business goals? Whether you are a Fortune 500 company or a small business, you want to align yourself with a company that is known for customer support and has a track record of customer success.
- *Reach*. Ensure that your perspective-retargeting platform has a seat on all major ad exchanges like Google's AdX, Facebook Exchange, and so on.
- *Technology*. Does the retargeting platform use their own technology or do they license others' as a middleman? You will want to align yourself with a company that has a focus on technology as this will provide your business a significant competitive advantage and ensure you are not spending your hard-earned money paying a middleman.
- *Flexibility*. Budgets can fluctuate, so you will want to go with a retargeting platform that can accommodate fluctuations and offer both insertion-order-based retargeting programs, but also have options with no contracts and no minimums.
- *Transparency*. Does the provider give insight into campaign metrics/ performance and optimize accordingly? Getting the most return on investment (ROI) is crucial. If your ads are not converting well on a particular site, you'll want to exclude that site from your campaigns. If your ads are not relevant to a certain region, you'll want to layer on geotargeting to make sure the right people see the right ads.
- *Service*. Is there someone you can call if you have questions or a problem?
- *Pricing*. Is there a dynamic-pricing model? Since retargeting is based on public auctions for impressions, fixed pricing can lead to suppliers arbitraging against you. Having a pricing model based on dynamic CPMs best aligns your business goals with your retargeting providers.

SETTING UP YOUR RETARGETING CAMPAIGN

Getting started with retargeting is easy. In its simplest form, retargeting only takes a few key steps. You will need to tag your website so it can start building lists of people to retarget. You will then need to create and upload ads to use in your retargeting campaign. From there, you can launch your campaign. Below, we've outlined all of the details that sit behind each of these steps.

Before You Get Started, Have a Privacy Policy on Your Website

Websites that need to collect personal information (for processing orders or newsletter signups, for example) need to include a privacy policy so users understand how their information will be used. This holds true for websites that run behavioral targeting or retargeting campaigns and need to provide visitors a place to opt out of this type of targeting.

This privacy policy should be hosted on your domain only. The link to your site's privacy policy should be clearly visible on all pages where you're collecting personal information—not just your homepage. A good practice is to provide a link to your privacy policy right below all forms where a visitor is entering their information, as well as in the footer. This will ensure your privacy policy is prominently visible to your visitors. The privacy policy should include the following information:

- A description of what personal information is collected.
- A description of how this information will be used by the company.
- A description of how this information will be transferred to third-party companies.
- Instructions on how users can modify or delete their personal information.
- Instructions on how users can opt out of future communications.
- Finally, websites that collect sensitive personal information, such as bank details and credit card numbers, must use a secure processing server (https://) when collecting this information.

If you are unsure of what to put in your privacy policy, it is recommended that you read some privacy policies on popular sites that you frequent, to get an idea of what is required. There are also some resources—such as www.iubenda.com/—that are helpful when creating your privacy policy. While advertisers are ultimately responsible for their own privacy policies and disclosures, please feel free to update your privacy policy with the following addendum:

As you browse [insert company website], advertising cookies will be placed on your computer so that we can understand what you are interested in. Our display advertising partner, AdRoll, then enables us to present you with retargeting advertising on other sites based on your previous interaction with [insert company website]. The techniques our partners employ do not collect personal information such as your name, e-mail address, postal address, or telephone number. You can visit this www.networkadvertising .org/choices/ to opt out of AdRoll and their partners' targeted advertising.

KICKING OFF YOUR RETARGETING CAMPAIGN

Tag Your Website

Before you start your retargeting program, you will need to first place a tag on your website. Single tags, like AdRoll's SmartTag, allow you

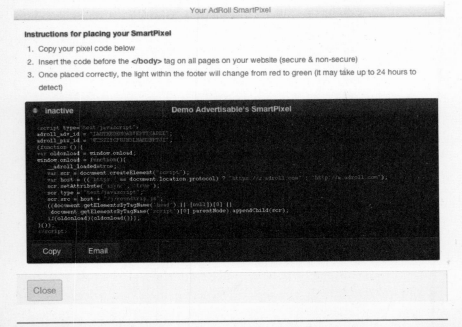

FIGURE 3.1   Sample Tag

to place a snippet of JavaScript across your website to give cookies to visitors who browse your site in order to later serve them your precisely targeted ads. Other platforms may require multiple tags.

Once you have a copy of the retargeting tag, you will need to implement it on your website. If you have access to your website's code, you will simply need to copy and paste the JavaScript before the </body> tag on all pages of your website.

If you are sending this to your developer, we recommend that you let him or her know to implement the code throughout the website before the </body> tag.

If you aren't sure that you implemented the retargeting tag correctly, just wait 24 hours, log in to your retargeting platform, and look at the Total Visitors list under Visitor Data.

If you have visitors in the list, then that means the tag is collecting data and was implemented correctly. You will need at least 500 visitors in your list before impressions can start serving.

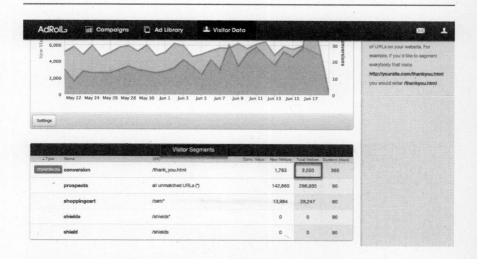

FIGURE 3.2   Understanding Visitor Segments

Set Your Targets!

Now that you have your website tagged and you have built your cookie pool, it is time to put retargeting into action. At the most basic level, you can retarget every visitor to your website with the same creative, but we recommend that you build out custom segments with different retargeting strategies. For example, you can create a shopping-cart-abandoners segment that retargets everyone who put items in a shopping cart but did not purchase with a free-shipping offer. Creating segments is simple.

To create a target segment:

Log into your retargeting platform and click on "Segment Visitors."

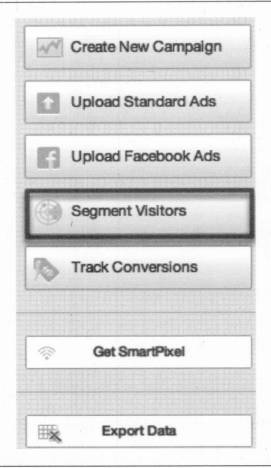

FIGURE 3.3   Segment Visitors

Once you are in the segmentation panel, you can name and create your segment based on a unique portion of your URL. For example, if you want to create a segment for your cart page (www.website.com/cart), you might name your segment cart and use the URL pattern/cart*. In this case, the asterisk represents a wildcard, allowing for variation after the unique aspect of the URL. Some popular segments include cart abandoners, specific products or product lines, and repeat-buyer segments.

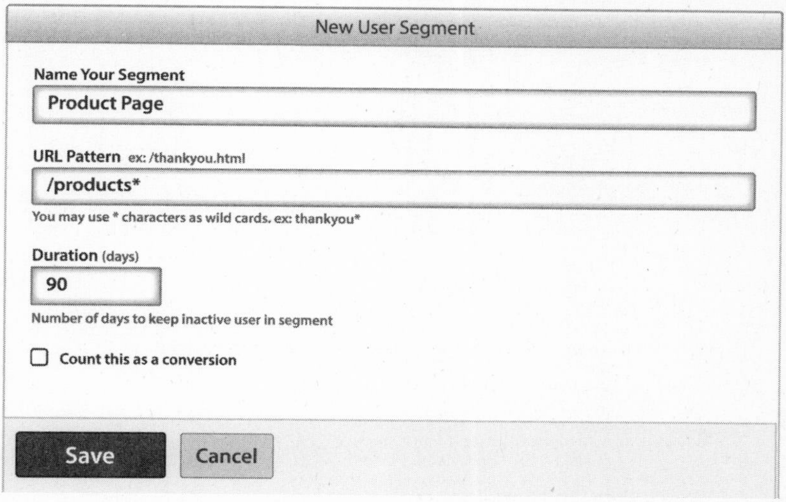

New User Segment

Name Your Segment

Product Page

URL Pattern ex: /thankyou.html

/products*

You may use * characters as wild cards. ex: thankyou*

Duration (days)

90

Number of days to keep inactive user in segment

☐ Count this as a conversion

Save   Cancel

FIGURE 3.4   Create User Segments

Track Your Conversions

Once you create segments, it is important to track conversions so you can measure the success of your retargeting program and optimize accordingly. It is up to you, the advertiser, to determine what you are going to track as conversions, but you know they are completed transactions as a result of an ad. Examples of conversions include: a purchase of a product or service, sign-up for a newsletter or lead form, or a user registering for a new account.

By incorporating conversion segments, you'll be able to track performance, identify your most profitable ads, measure ROI, and remove converted users from your retargeting campaign and put them in a separate flow for repeat buyers.

To properly track conversions, you will need to create a conversion segment in your retargeting platform. No additional website tagging will be needed. To do this, click on Track Conversions in your retargeting platform, then name and create the conversion tracking, based on the portion of the URL.

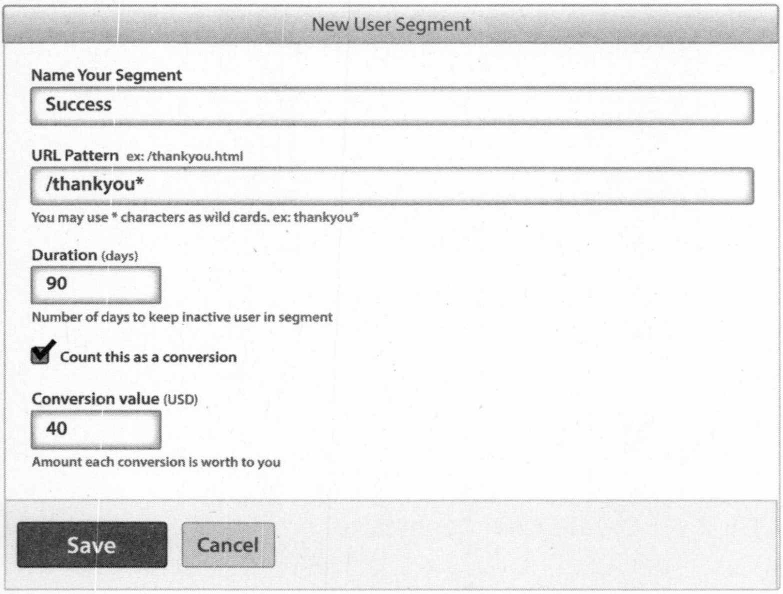

FIGURE 3.5   Tracking Conversions

Upload Your Retargeting Ads

Before launching your retargeting campaign, you need to have ads. There are 10 ad types that are typically used in retargeting. If you are just getting started, we recommend starting with the five major ad types, which provide ample coverage across all major exchanges, including FBX.

Major Ad Types

FIGURE 3.6   Sample 300×250 Ad Unit

FIGURE 3.7   Sample 160×600 Ad Unit

FIGURE 3.8   Sample 728×90 Ad Unit

FIGURE 3.9   100×72 Facebook Right-Hand Side

FIGURE 3.10   200×200 Facebook News Feed

Ads can be Flash or they can be static. If they are Flash, make sure they are no longer than 30 seconds (at 15 to 20 frames per second), after which point they remain static. Also make sure all ads have a 1×1 border around the edge. For more details on creative requirements and best practices, please see Chapter 6.

Launch Your Retargeting Campaign!

Once your ads are uploaded, approved, and your targets set, you can launch your retargeting campaign. It is important to monitor performance, or to work with a provider that will track and optimize your campaigns for you.

SELLING RETARGETING INTERNALLY

There is only so much budget available at a company and new initiatives often have to fight harder to get that money than incumbent programs. In a perfect world, every company would employee the 80/20 budget rule that the book *Complete B2B Online Marketing* suggests, in which companies save 20 percent of their budget for innovation. If your company saves a portion of its budget for testing new ideas then you are all set. Leverage that innovation budget to test retargeting and prove its success. Then you can move retargeting into a core program and fund it to maximize ROI-positive returns. If your organization does not reserve a portion of budget for testing, then getting funding may be more difficult, but by no means will it be impossible.

According to a recent study, 87 percent of advertisers say that retargeting is important or very important to their marketing strategy.[1]

Show that to your management chain to help you determine what programs will need to help fund retargeting. When looking for program funding, start with business goals. If your organization goals

---

[1]References AdRoll's 2014 state of the retargeting industry benchmark report.

involve sales or growth then retargeting is a great fit. For example, Nitro PDF saw an 18 percent increase in online sales after implementing retargeting. Traditional advertising efforts are much harder to track and metric, so if you work for a company that runs offline-marketing efforts, try to work with those teams to fund your retargeting efforts. If your organization runs traditional display ads, getting funding for a retargeting program should be easy. According to a study, advertisers said that retargeting performed as good or better than other forms of display. New Relic, an application performance management and monitoring company and retargeting users, has also seen retargeting costs per acquisitions at 44 percent lower than other forms of display advertising.

Working with a media team to fund retargeting is a great way to help drive a strong ROI for online advertising programs and both parties win.

If you are a small-business owner, it is less about what team you partner with to fund retargeting and more about driving business results. Los Angeles-based tea importer and wholesaler, The Art of Tea, with 70,000 monthly unique visitors, decided to try out retargeting to promote their Summer Iced Tea line and build brand familiarity and loyalty for their later tea lines during the peak season of winter. They launched a shopping-cart-specific campaign to target customers who placed an item in their online-shopping cart, but did not complete the purchase. By doing this, they generated a 5× return on investment and helped to achieve top-line business objectives.

TIPS TO WIN BUDGET

1. Whenever trying to get funding for a marketing program, make sure it aligns with business goals.
2. If growth and sales are important to your business, then retargeting is a great solution to test and implement.
3. Use case studies, facts, and industry research to help build your case.

4. Partner with other teams that have similar objectives and use retargeting as a win for everyone.

GETTING STARTED WITH B2C RETARGETING AND THE SHOPPING CART

Retargeting can be used by almost any vertical. The earliest adopters of retargeting were e-commerce sites. Capturing the elusive shopping cart abandoner has kept many an e-commerce manager up at night. Then came retargeting. It was a way to reengage with people who spent time browsing a website and making the extra effort to put something in a shopping cart, but walked away. Yes, this is just one of many use cases for retargeting, but for many this is the one that started it all.

Why Do People Abandon Their Carts?

Forrester Research reports that on average only 3 percent of shoppers make a purchase during their first visit to an online store. Of the remaining 97 percent, 71 percent place an item in their shopping cart but end up abandoning. So what are the top reasons they're hesitant to buy?

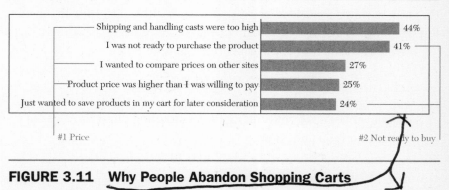

FIGURE 3.11   Why People Abandon Shopping Carts

Source: Adapted from Forrester Research, www.forrester.com/Understanding+Shopping+Cart +Abandonment/fulltext/-/E-RES56827.

Price and *timing* are the leading factors for cart abandonment. While typical conversion-optimization practices—such as testing different versions of carts, testing checkout flows, being up front with shipping details, and reducing anxiety by signaling trust—can increase conversions, these practices won't address the biggest causes of abandonment.

Fortunately, display retargeting can help address customer concerns over price and message them when they are ready to buy.

HOW TO SET UP A SHOPPING CART ABANDONMENT RETARGETING CAMPAIGN

Segment Shopping Cart Abandoners

You can launch a shopping cart abandonment campaign by creating a segment of visitors who visit your shopping cart page or interact with your shopping cart, and then filtering out visitors who already converted. What you're left with is a segment of visitors who added something to their cart, but did not complete their purchase.

Determine How Long to Target Cart Abandoners

Customers think about and comparison shop different products for different amounts of time. Customers make considerations around buying products with a bigger price tag (for example, furniture, electronics, etc.) for a longer time than lower price-per-unit products (for example, apparel, cosmetics, etc.).

You should be trying to reach potential customers as soon as they abandon, but the length of time you should target abandoners should be determined by how long the typical sale and consideration cycle takes for your customers. You can get some idea of this timing from a days-to-purchase report in Google Analytics.

The report below shows a longer purchase consideration cycle with almost 12 percent of sales happening 60 days after the first visit.

Days to Purchase	Transactions	Percentage of all purchases
0 days	3,598	59.31%
1 day	198	3.26%
2 days	155	2.56%
3 days	102	1.68%
4 days	80	1.32%
5 days	65	1.07%
6 days	57	0.94%
7 days	68	1.12%
8–14 days	256	4.22%
15–30 days	379	6.25%
31–60 days	382	6.30%
61–120 days	425	7.01%
121–365 days	301	4.96%

FIGURE 3.12　Days to Purchase

Static Creative versus Personalized Creative

AdRoll often sees great results from retargeting campaigns with static-branded ads, but personalized creative can also be very effective. Sometimes all it takes to push someone over the edge and make a purchase is to remind them of the great merchandise they were previously interested in purchasing. Using dynamic creative, such as LiquidAds, you can remind abandoners of products at a later stage in their decision-making process.

Shipping Promotions

In 2011, data from Shop.org's *The State of Retailing Online* indicated that 77 percent of consumers said free shipping would encourage them to purchase more products online. In comparison, 56 percent cited free returns as the second most-popular feature. Highlighting offers such as free shipping and returns in your retargeting ads can often be the extra push needed for abandoners to convert.

Discount

Customers love a deal and offering a discount is the easiest way to address concerns customers have over the cost of merchandise.

USE A MULTISTAGE RETARGETING CAMPAIGN

You don't want to encourage shoppers to abandon their carts just to receive promotional offers and discounts, so if you plan on using promotional retargeting to help convert customers, you should use a multistage retargeting campaign to maximize profit.

This means showing a less promotional message to visitors who abandon throughout most of their purchase consideration, and then getting

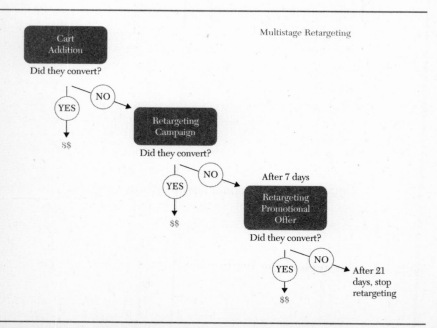

FIGURE 3.13   Example of a Multistage Campaign

more aggressive with your offer at a point in time when you think it is the only way to capture the remaining abandoners.

RETARGETING FOR B2B

Although most of the early adopters of retargeting were B2C companies, retargeting has exploded in the B2B industry as a must have throughout the customer lifecycle. With a longer sales cycle and multiple touch points as the norms in B2B marketing, retargeting plays a role in the entire funnel. From awareness to consideration to purchase and onboarding, retargeting can be used to acquire new leads, influence, speed up the purchase cycle, and educate customers. We will go into more advanced retargeting strategies in Chapter 7, but here are some ways B2B marketers can use retargeting to acquire leads.

FORM ABANDONERS

Form abandonment is to the B2B marketer what cart abandonment is to the B2C marketer. Online-lead generation is at the crux of any business-to-business marketing strategy, but on average 95 percent of people don't fill out a form on their first visit. The conversion-optimization industry has done a great job at teaching online marketing how to improve form completion rate, but the reality is the vast majority of people will never complete a form on your website. This is where retargeting comes into play.

CREATING FORM-ABANDONER SEGMENTS

Custom segments are central in B2B retargeting and the form-abandoner segment is a great place to start your retargeting efforts. Log into your retargeting platform and create a custom segment of visitors that have reached your form page, but have not reached the thank you page. If you have multiple-offer types, we recommend creating custom segments for each offer type so you create customer messaging for each offer.

TEST MESSAGING

If you are a B2B-tech website and you have a demo offer, a free-trial offer, and an industry white-paper offer you should create two different retargeting segments so you can message each group appropriately. For someone who has abandoned the demo form, entice them to come back and complete their information. You can also create a multi-stage retargeting campaign that will rotate in different offer types. For example, if a visitor saw a demo form and did not complete it, retarget them with a demo offer for seven days. After seven days, if that prospect still doesn't complete a form, rotate in messaging around your free white paper. After seven days, rotate in an offer for a free consultation to see if that entices a response.

RETARGET RESPONSIBLY

Now that you know the basics of getting started with retargeting, you should be ready to launch your first campaign. Throughout out the rest of this book we will walk you through various best practices, strategies, and tips to make your programs even more successful.

CHAPTER 4

Smart Targeting

Reach the Right People at the Right Time

KNOW YOUR CUSTOMERS

When ad exchanges began to dominate the display advertising ecosystem, and cookie-based ad targeting started to mature, marketers were able to shift their focus from "what sites should I target?" to "which web users are most valuable for my brand?" The old playbook was thrown out, and a new breed of online advertising was born. This new approach is called online behavioral advertising (OBA). It relies on the cookie technology that we described earlier, but it is a much more granular and targeted approach.

Marketing is all about reaching the right customers with the right message at the optimal time. OBA gives marketers a new toolset to do so. In order to accomplish this, a marketer needs to understand who his or her potential customers are, how they behave, and, ultimately, what it's going to take to turn them into customers. This is something that good marketers have always known. But cookie-based tracking gave them the ability to build much richer profiles for their current customers and potential customers. Before you can act, you have to analyze, so the first step in building an effective retargeting strategy is to truly understand your customers.

There are a number of tools that will help you learn about your customers. Analytics products allow you to identify purchase paths, analyze funnels, and identify trends. Most of them are centered around optimizing your website, pinpointing potential problem areas that are leading to drop-off points, or assessing marketing-campaign performance. Some of the more advanced tools allow you to see where customers are clicking or mousing with heat maps, which is valuable when trying to pinpoint intent signals.

While these tools are invaluable and should be a major component of any marketer's toolkit, marketers should take additional measures to understand their potential customers and what it is going to take to turn them into purchasers.

Live chat is an incredible way to connect with your customers on a daily basis. You get to hear what they are asking for and care about, learn their pain points, and adjust your approach accordingly. In essence, by introducing live chat, you're giving your potential customers a direct line of communication to your team while they are in the process of evaluating your brand or products. It's an incredibly powerful way to gain access to their thought process when they are shopping. There are a number of very simple-to-install live chat tools, but my favorite is Olark, which can be found at www.olark.com.

Similarly, combing through customer-service e-mails is a great way to stay connected to your customers. What topics are brought up most often in customer-service e-mails? What questions come up most frequently? Knowing and understanding all of this won't just make you a more effective marketer, it will make the company stronger in general.

In order to begin crafting a retargeting strategy, you need to understand how customers interact with your site, what they care about, and what it's going to take to get them over the purchase hump. Once you understand this, you can get the right message in front of the right people at the right time. But without this knowledge, you won't be able to identify the actions your customers are taking that indicate that they are ready to make a purchase.

IDENTIFYING INTENT SIGNALS

Every company is going to value different actions as intent signals. An intent signal is something that the potential customer does that signals, "I'm interested in this product or service." It could be they opened a specific marketing e-mail or filled out a lead-generation form. It could be they visited a specific product page or watched a certain webinar. Or it could be as overt as actually placing an item in their shopping cart. The point is, these intent signals are going to be unique to your business, your sales cycle, and your customers.

Diving into your data will reveal some of these intent signals. How much more likely is someone to purchase after they've looked at three products versus just one? What is the conversion rate of customers who checked to see if the item was available in their size versus those who just viewed a product page? What is the average order value of a customer who comes from Facebook versus one who comes from a paid search ad? Yes, digging into these types of metrics is a more advanced approach, and these are the types of things that the savviest marketers are thinking about while identifying intent signals. But there are some much more basic approaches to identifying intent signals that are very powerful, so don't get overwhelmed. We'll cover those shortly.

Once you understand these signals, you can craft your audience-segmentation strategy. Audience segmentation is simply how you slice and dice your potential customers into buckets in order to market to them.

When getting started with retargeting, you want to start broad and then drill down into more targeted audiences as you learn what's working. Let's outline some basic strategies to get you started.

FUNNEL-BASED SEGMENTATION

A very simple but powerful segmentation strategy is to create segments for the different steps in your sales funnel. If you are an e-commerce apparel store, your funnel may look like this:

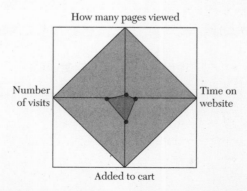

FIGURE 4.1 Sample Intent Signals and How They Play a Role in Establishing User's Propensity to Buy

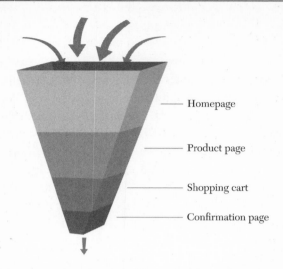

Homepage

Product page

Shopping cart

Confirmation page

FIGURE 4.2   A Common Buyer Journey Is When a Website Visitor Goes to Your Homepage Followed by a Product-Specific Page. The Visitor Then Places the Product in a Shopping Cart, Goes to That Shopping Cart, Checks Out, and Receives a Confirmation Page.

If so, you might create the following segments:

- All site visitors.
- People viewed at least one product page.
- People who put something in their shopping cart.
- People who successfully purchased something.

Type	Segment Name	URL	Total Users	Duration (Days)	Target or Exclude	
	All Visitors	all unmatched URLs (*)	84,400	90	Target ⬤ Exclude	⊗
	male_shoppers	/mens_clothing	30,056	90	Target ⬤ Exclude	⊗
	male_shoppers_pants	/mens_clothing/pants	18,868	90	Target ⬤ Exclude	⊗
	male_shoppers_shirts	/mens_clothing/shirts	11,188	90	Target ⬤ Exclude	⊗
	female_shoppers	/womens_clothing	54,344	90	Target ⬤ Exclude	⊗
	female_shoppers_pants	/womens_clothing/pants	14,113	90	Target ⬤ Exclude	⊗
	female_shoppers_shirts	/womens_clothing/shirts	16,234	90	Target ⬤ Exclude	⊗
	female_shoppers_jackets	/womens_clothing/jackets	21,997	90	Target ⬤ Exclude	⊗
	shopping_cart	/cart	18,871	90	Target ⬤ Exclude	⊗
Conversion	purchase_complete	/thankyou	12,113	90	Target ⬤ Exclude	⊗

FIGURE 4.3   User Segments in First Example

This simple approach allows you to run a few different campaigns that will drive potential customers through the funnel along the purchase path. With these four segments, you can run campaigns that keep your brand top of mind for window shoppers. Or recapture shopping-cart abandoners by targeting people who put something in their cart but did not complete the purchase. You could also re-engage past purchasers by running a campaign to the group that already purchased something a couple of weeks after the purchase event occurred. Even with these basic segments, you can craft a retargeting strategy that will drastically improve your overall conversion rates.

Skullcandy Uses Custom Segments to Drive Sales

Skullcandy wanted to smartly target their audience to drive greater ROI so they segmented visitors based on intent levels. They did this so they could prioritize budget for the highest-intent users and also to create specific messaging that would drive conversions among people who had a longer evaluation cycle. One sample segment that Skullcandy used to capture high-intent purchasers was around visitors who came to the website within 1 to 14 days and retarget them with ads on both standard display and Facebook Exchange. Within that segment, Skullcandy excluded visitors who had purchased.

CATEGORY-BASED SEGMENTATION

You can take this approach to the next level by breaking out segments based on the categories that people have browsed on your site. Every site is going to have a different way of categorizing products or offerings. Take a look at your site map, and figure out how your traffic is divided. Remember to start broad.

A very simple example of this in retail is breaking out men's products from women's. Often a site that caters to both men and women has separate, clearly defined purchase paths for these two groups. This is a very broad approach to segmentation, but it allows you to immediately offer up a more tailored advertisement to these two groups. It also allows you to announce new products that may apply to one gender only without wasting marketing budget on the other gender.

Take this a step further by breaking out different product categories into segments. Let's say that you are the marketing manager for an online fashion store that sells both men's and women's clothes. Your segmentation strategy might include the previously described funnel segments, with the following additions:

- All site visitors
- Male shoppers
- Male pants shoppers
- Male shirt shoppers
- Male jacket shoppers
- Female shoppers
- Female pants shoppers
- Female shirt shoppers
- Female jacket shoppers
- Shopping-cart page visitors
- Purchasers

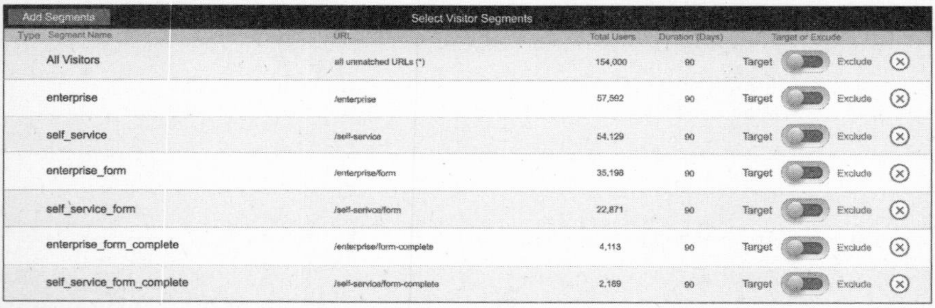

FIGURE 4.4   User Segments in Second Example

It's important to note that you need enough traffic to support this level of segmentation. If your site has only a few thousand unique visitors a month, you will want to stick to the simple funnel segmentation strategy described previously. However, if this strategy is viable for your site, it allows you to serve significantly more targeted ads through the purchase process. It also enables cross selling. For example, if someone purchased a pair of pants, you could use this strategy to offer them complementary products, like a shirt. Or, if you have excess inventory in a given category, you can use this strategy to push that inventory to people who have already exhibited an interested in those product types. The point is, by segmenting your audience in this way, you can make sure that you are messaging potential customers with advertisements relevant to their interests.

A business-to-business example of this might be slicing your customer base by product lines or customer segments. For example, your company may offer enterprise clients a separate set of products from what you offer self-serve clients. You may have a completely different purchase path for these two customer segments, with different pricing tiers, and varied promotional offers. Chances are you have a sign-up flow for self-service customers, and a lead-generation form for enterprise clients. You probably also have a different cost per acquisition (CPA) that you're willing to pay for each of these customer segments because they may have a very different lifetime value for your company.

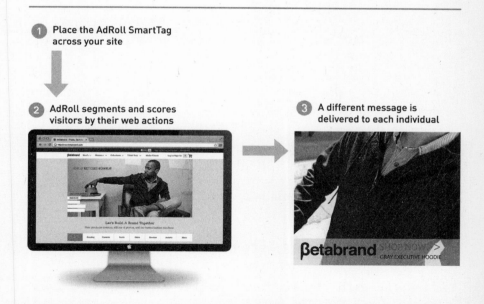

FIGURE 4.5   Here Are Different Customer Paths for Two Different Customer Segments.

In that case, you may want to create the following segments:

- All site visitors
- Enterprise offer for page visitors
- Self-serve offer for page visitors
- Enterprise-lead form for page visitors
- Sign-up now for page visitors
- Enterprise-lead form complete
- Self-serve successful sign up

Type Segment Name	URL	Total Users	Duration (Days)	Target or Exclude	
All Visitors	all unmatched URLs (*)	154,000	90	Target ◉ Exclude	⊗
enterprise	/enterprise	57,592	90	Target ◉ Exclude	⊗
self_service	/self-service	54,129	90	Target ◉ Exclude	⊗
enterprise_form	/enterprise/form	35,198	90	Target ◉ Exclude	⊗
self_service_form	/self-service/form	22,871	90	Target ◉ Exclude	⊗
enterprise_form_complete	/enterprise/form-complete	4,113	90	Target ◉ Exclude	⊗
self_service_form_complete	/self-service/form-complete	2,189	90	Target ◉ Exclude	⊗

FIGURE 4.6   User Segments in Example Above

By segmenting your customers as such, you can begin to implement something called *lead nurturing*. Lead nurturing is simply using marketing to engage customers as they travel along the purchase path. Often with B2B products, potential customers are shopping around and comparing you to your competitors. By implementing a segmentation strategy that enables lead nurturing, you can ensure that your brand stays in front of those potential customers while they do this research.

PRODUCT-BASED SEGMENTATION

If your site has the traffic and product stock keeping units (SKUs) to support it, product-based segmentation is a great way to ensure that your ads are highly personalized. Product-based segmentation is segmenting your customers based on the specific products that they viewed.

It is important to note that this particular type of segmentation is not appropriate for every company. This really works best for companies with a smaller number of products (less than 20 for example) and enough traffic to populate each product-based segment with a meaningful amount of potential customers (let's say 5,000 unique visitors per product per month).

We've seen this work most effectively in B2B companies with a handful of offerings, or e-commerce sites dedicated to a specific product set. For simplicity's sake, let's take Rickshaw Bags as an example—they sell urban-commuter bags made in their San Francisco headquarters. Rickshaw Bags might set up the following segments for each of their most popular products.

- All site visitors
- Zero Messenger Bag page visitors
- Commuter Laptop Bag page visitors
- Velo Backpack page visitors
- Shopping cart visitors
- Purchasers

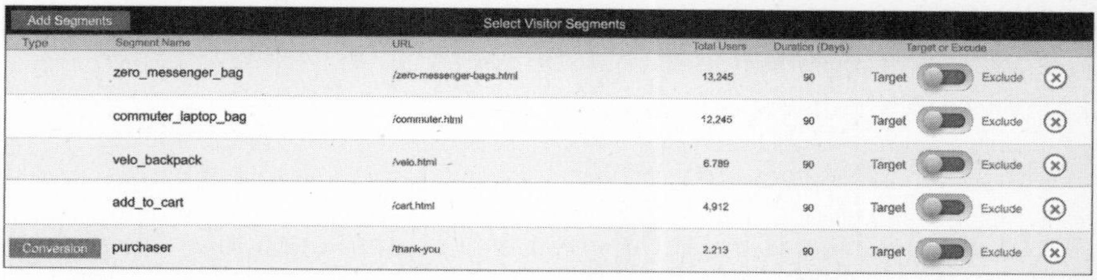

FIGURE 4.7   Sample Rickshaw Bags Segments

This would allow Rickshaw Bags to focus their messaging on the specific products that potential customers are browsing. As they run promotions around different products, Rickshaw would be able to engage people that they know are in the market for that product, and guarantee that their marketing dollars are being directed towards those site browsers who are most likely to purchase that product.

This strategy might be a bit cumbersome for online retailers or apparel sites that have hundreds or thousands of products. Obviously, setting up and managing segments for each of these products would be time consuming and tedious, which is why dynamic creative is a much better way for these types of sites to accomplish this highly personalized interaction with customers on the product level. Dynamic creative is when the ad content changes based on the specific web user being targeted. We'll cover this in detail in Chapter 7.

ADVANCED SEGMENTATION TECHNIQUES

Some of the more robust retargeting providers will support more advanced forms of segmentation. Often, there is a correlation between how many pages a customer browses and their likelihood to purchase. For argument's sake, let's assume that during your marketing analysis you discover that customers who view at least three pages on your site complete a purchase at a 20 percent higher rate. This would mean that the number of pages viewed could be a pretty powerful intent signal. If this is the case for your customer base you could employ a segmentation strategy as follows:

- All site visitors
- Visitors who browsed at least three pages
- Visitors who put something in the shopping cart
- Purchasers

In essence, this is just a different way of thinking about a sales funnel. In this case, the intent signal that you are valuing is the number of pages visited, rather than a visit to a specific step in your sales process, like in the first example of this chapter.

This approach can become even more powerful if taken a step further. Let's go back to the marketing analysis that uncovered the correlation between the number of pages visited by a customer and the conversion rate. Empowered by the increase in ROI you've achieved from your new segmentation strategy, you dig deeper and discover that customers who visited three or more product-specific pages not only have a higher conversion rate, but also the average order value of their purchase is 30 percent higher. Now you are starting to focus on not only those users who are most likely to convert, but also those who are going to spend the most. In that case, you'd create the following segments:

- All site visitors
- Visitors who browsed at least three pages
- Visitors who browsed at least three product-specific pages
- Visitors who put something in the shopping cart
- Purchasers

In certain cases, your site might have far too many pages, or far too many categories, for it to be practical to create segments for everything that you're interested in tracking. For the more advanced marketer with access to software engineers, there is a technique in which key-value pairs can be passed into the retargeting tag on your site (often called a pixel). A key-value pair is simply two linked data items. For example, the key might be product category and the value might be men's pants. As a marketer, if you're able to pass key-value pairs into the pixel, then you can create some very interesting segments.

Let's take the Rickshaw Bags example again. Rickshaw Bags looks at their data and realizes that customers tend to purchase different products of the same color and material, because they match. For example, someone who purchases a tweed laptop bag will often purchase a tweed iPad sleeve. Being based in San Francisco, their marketing team knows that customers who have purchased one item in San Francisco Giants Orange are very likely going to purchase other items in San Francisco Giants Orange as they become available. (San Francisco Giants fans are like that.) So Chris, the marketing guru at Rickshaw, begins capturing things like the material and the color of the items purchased in his retargeting tag.

Then, as the baseball playoffs are approaching and Rickshaw Bags creates a new accessory for the most recently released smartphone, Chris is able to create a segment consisting of everyone who has purchased Giants Orange products in the past, and then market that item to those customers.

CRM SEGMENTS

A very exciting new form of retargeting is something called *CRM retargeting*. CRM, which stands for Customer Relationship Management, is a system that manages customer information and interaction with a business.

CRM retargeting allows you to leverage offline-customer data to reach customers online with targeted ads. In essence, CRM retargeting allows you to take a list of e-mail addresses and associate a cookie with those e-mails in order to target them throughout the web. It's really powerful for reengaging past purchasers or promoting a sale to people who haven't been to your site recently.

Let's say that you operate a site that sells outdoor apparel. You ran a sale for Memorial Day that went very well, and you were able to capture the e-mail addresses of everyone who purchased during that sale. Now, you are going to run a similar sale for Labor Day. By leveraging CRM retargeting, you can upload those e-mail addresses to your retargeting provider, and engage those people who purchased during the Memorial Day sale with ads promoting the Labor Day sale.

As a marketer, there is probably customer data that you keep track of in your database or CRM platform that you cannot capture simply by tracking customer-site behavior. CRM retargeting allows you to tap into that. As another example, let's pretend that you run marketing for a company that sells software on an annual-license model. You may keep track of when customers' licenses expire in your CRM. Your boss has come to you with the goal of increasing license-renewal rates over the next six months. With CRM retargeting, you could create a segment of users whose license was set to expire within 30 days, and run a campaign targeting that group. The beauty of CRM retargeting is that it doesn't require that the user has visited your site recently. It just requires that you have the user's e-mail address.

The segmentation strategy that's right for you depends on the product or service that you sell, your customers, and your goals. It's important to make sure that you have enough site traffic to support the strategy that you select, which is why we generally say that you should start out broadly with funnel-based segmentation, and then move to one of the more granular segmentation strategies as you become more familiar with retargeting.

CHAPTER 5

Taking Your Retargeting to the Next Level

Optimization Strategies That Work

Retargeting, much like other modern response-oriented marketing channels, is not a set-it-and-forget-it proposition. Some strategies will work and other won't. Campaigns that hit performance goals initially can decay over time without the necessary attention. Campaigns that don't work can be tweaked to bring them up to required levels. Even stable campaigns can be enhanced proactively to ensure you're making the most from every marketing dollar.

This is where the optimization process comes in. The best retargeting account managers usually have an optimization checklist that they work through when trying to enhance campaign performance. This checklist is probably different depending on the vertical and site traffic of the account that they're working on. However, we can boil down optimization strategies to a few universal concepts that can usually be applied to any campaign.

FREQUENCY CAPS

Frequency cap is a term used specially in the online advertising world that refers to the number of times a user is shown an ad. For example, if there is a frequency cap of three impressions per day, that particular user can see a maximum of three of your ads in a 24-hour period.

Frequency caps are important in the retargeting world to both prevent ad burnout, which is discussed in more detail in Chapter 6, and to prevent users from becoming overwhelmed by your ads. The right frequency cap will vary by industry and by goal. For example, if you are a daily deals site, setting a frequency cap of 20 impressions per month won't work, as the offer is valid for a short period of time. In this case, six impressions per day may be a better starting point.

The best way to determine the right frequency cap is by looking at the data. If you have access to the right metrics, users will tell you by their behavior what the frequency cap should be. Here's an example of what this data can look like:

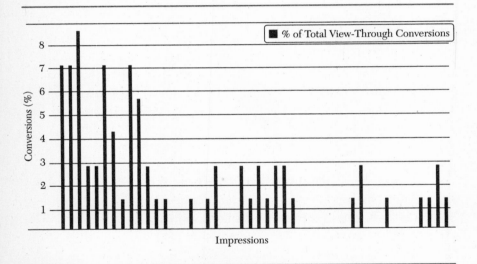

FIGURE 5.1   Example of What the Data Looks Like to Determine Frequency Cap

This graph shows the percent of conversions that occur from a campaign on the y-axis after each number of impressions on the x-axis. As you can see from this graph, after about 13 impressions, a small percent of conversions take place. In fact, about 60 percent of the conversions happen after the first 13 impressions. This does not necessarily mean to cut off the campaign after 13 impressions— 40 percent is still a big chunk of conversions. However, if this advertiser is spending more than 40 percent of their budget on impressions that occur after the thirteenth impression, then that budget isn't being spent efficiently.

In lieu of setting hard frequency caps, one technique that sophisticated retargeting platforms use is to employ a bidding strategy called *cadence modification*. This is when the bidding algorithm automatically bids less on each subsequent impression. The theory indicates that the first impression is worth more than the second impression, which is worth more than the third, and so on. A high-numbered impression isn't worthless, you just might not want to pay a lot for it. By slightly decreasing the bid with each impression, you end up with a more dynamic frequency cap because you'll win fewer high-frequency auctions.

This type of bidding strategy is usually baked into the algorithm of the platform you use to execute your retargeting and isn't something you'd set manually. Therefore, it's usually best to ask your provider how frequency is factored into the algorithm, and you can still use hard frequency caps in conjunction with cadence modification depending on the specific needs of your business.

AUDIENCE DURATION

The cousin of frequency cap is audience duration. When creating your retargeting campaigns, you select who you are going to target based on segmentation, and also *when* you want to target those people. The most common cookie duration is 30 days after their most recent visit to the site, but that may not be ideal for everyone. For example, if you have a 60-day buying cycle, you may want to set your cookie window to 60 days rather than 30. On the flip side, if you have a short buying cycle then you may want to set your cookie window to 15 days and stop your advertising after that point as it will become less effective.

Similar to frequency cap, the best way to determine audience duration is by looking at the actual data. Here's another example of a histogram that shows the percent of conversions that happen after each subsequent day.

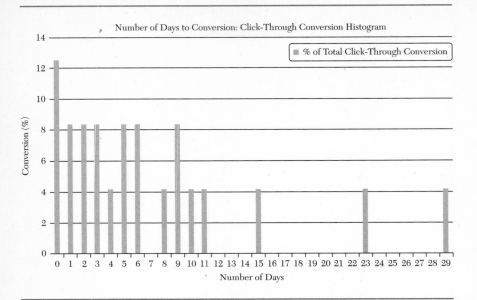

FIGURE 5.2   Conversion Histogram Showing the Percentage of Conversions that Happen Each Day

As you can see in this graph, there's a tremendous drop-off after about 11 days. Again, that's not to say that you don't want to target people after longer durations, you just might want to set up different campaigns that you manage differently.

Similar to frequency cap, many sophisticated retargeting bidders automatically factor recency into their bidding algorithm. This way, you're automatically bidding more for impressions to users who have showed interest most recently.

SEGMENT PRIORITIZATION

In general, optimization is a process of targeting more intelligently. Thinking about segmentation strategy is a great way to accomplish this. Through segmentation, you can decide if there are people who you don't want to target, or if there are people who you're not targeting who you should.

For example, a typical group of users that you might want to segment out for a period of time is people who complete a purchase. Depending on your product, once they purchase something, they might not need it for a certain amount of time. These are people who you might want to negatively target or filter out of your retargeting campaigns for a certain amount of time.

Similarly, you then might want to create a loyalty segment of past purchasers to target differently. An example of this would be targeting people who purchased but haven't been back to the site in 30 days. These could be great people to make aware of a new product line, a sale you're having, or a new feature you roll out.

Once you start getting the hang of positive and negative segmentation, you'll probably find other opportunities. For example, if you're an online retailer, you might not want to target product ads to people who visit your jobs page.

CREATIVE TESTING

Chapter 6 goes into greater detail on creative best practices; however, having an ad testing and creative-refresh strategy is critical for both sustaining and improving performance over time.

Ideally, for every campaign, there should be at least two creatives running. After sufficient data is generated, the winner stays live, and the loser is replaced by a new challenger. This process of A/B testing provides a manageable way of constantly learning about what works and what doesn't to improve performance over time.

If creative resources are scarce (which they usually are) it's okay to test smaller things and schedule larger changes further apart. For example, even testing calls to action, like click here versus buy now, can have a big impact on click-through rates and ultimately campaign performance.

INVENTORY MANAGEMENT

Frequency caps, audience duration, segmentation, and creative address the who, what, and when of optimization, but the actual sites the ads run on is the where. When you consider that a retargeting platform will often have access to tens of thousands of websites (if not more) on which to deliver ads, the opportunity to manage those websites becomes obvious. Some sites perform better for some brands than others, some ad spaces perform better than others. In general, it's best to start with the broadest reach possible in order to generate data. However, after a campaign has run for a fair amount of time, there's often opportunity to look at performance by ad space and start weeding out low performers.

To accomplish this, you'll need to sort the ad spaces by number of impressions to ensure you're not pulling out ad spaces that just haven't gotten enough traffic yet. However, if there are extremely low performers among the group of ad spaces that have statistically relevant data, it makes perfect sense to pull them out so those impressions can be allocated to higher-performing placements.

RETARGETING TIPS FOR TRAVEL AND BACK TO SCHOOL

We wanted to provide you with some practical tips for different verticals and high-volume time periods throughout the course of this book. Below you will find how to take your back-to-school retargeting programs to the next level. You will also find tips for driving incremental sales in the travel industry.

TIPS FOR MAXIMIZING BACK-TO-SCHOOL MARKETING

The back-to-school shopping season is the second-highest consumer spending event of the year (behind the holidays), and a great time to increase online sales using retargeting—if you haven't already started. According to a recent study by the National Retail Foundation (NRF), back-to-school and back-to-college spending combined is expected to reach $72.5 billion during the 2013 school year.

Families with school-age children will spend an average of $634.78 on apparel, shoes, supplies, and electronics, while college students preparing for their return to independence will spend a whopping $836.83 on average. The NRF also notes that 70 percent of consumers will begin their shopping within one week to one month of school starting—now is the time to begin marketing to your potential customers.[1]

---

[1]www.nrf.com/modules.php?name=News&op=viewlive&sp_id=1626.

Retargeting creative needs to create value. According to the NRF, this season there will be more people comparison shopping online and these savvy shoppers will be looking for sales. So be sure to use creative that includes promotions, sales, and other offers like free shipping.

FIGURE 5.3   Shop.ca Creates Value with Its Ads by Offering Savvy Back-to-School Shoppers Up to Half-Off on Essentials

Source: Reproduced by permission of Matthew Growden.

Look at ways to reward your most loyal shoppers. For example, create a segment of past purchasers and retarget them with discounts on popular products.

Retargeting in the Facebook Newsfeed is also highly effective at driving back-to-school sales. These ad units are prominent and they come with a viral effect if people are encouraged to like, share, and comment on the ads.

A QUICK TRIP TO SUCCESSFUL TRAVEL RETARGETING

With 61 percent of users researching their travel plans online, and 51 percent booking online,[2] brands are constantly vying to stay top of

---

[2]www.emarketer.com/Article.aspx?R=1008706&ecid=a6506033675d47f881651943c21c5ed4.

mind for consumers. Retargeting is a great way to differentiate your travel site and keep it top of mind for your perspective buyers.

Tip 1: The Buying Window for Large-Ticket Items Is Longer Than You Think

We've noticed customers who scope high-price-point products or long-travel distances generally convert several weeks, or even months, after the initial visit to the website. For larger-ticket items, make sure you set your cookie window to a longer time frame so you don't miss out when customers are ready to buy.

Tip 2: Follow Up Your Contextual Display Campaigns with Retargeting

What's the right mix?

The travel industry is highly seasonal, with many travel companies spending significant budget on contextually targeted display campaigns to promote the brand. Retargeting should be used in accordance with these programs as retargeting is a great closer. Make sure your ads also have a strong call to action.

Tip 3: Keep Retargeting On in the Off Season

Although traffic dips during the off season for many travel sites, it is important to keep retargeting on so you can convert those off-season buyers. Incorporate discounts and pricing-focused messaging to entice visitors to buy.

Tip 4: Keep Testing Creative

If you don't want to offer a discount in your ads, try showing people something they haven't seen. Let them know about nearby attractions, delicious cuisine, or seasonal events to bring them back to your site. Also vary and test the call-to-actions to see what resonates with your audience. For example, Hipmunk Hotels & Flights ran campaigns for their updated hotel search product by testing different messaging to drive the best conversion rates.[3]

FIGURE 5.4   Hipmunk Tested Different Messaging in Their Ads to Maximize Results

FIGURE 5.5   Another Example of Creative Testing

CONCLUSION

Regardless of what vertical you are in, we hope you've learned more about how frequency caps and inventory management can help drive success for your retargeting programs. We'll also go into more advanced strategies as the book progresses.

---

[3]Originally published on http://blog.adroll.com/travel-marketing.

CHAPTER **6**

Creative Best Practices

Good creative can make or break any marketing campaign. How do you know what is going to compel action, drive engagement, and ultimately convert a user, especially when you are building a program from the ground up? As the saying goes, good artists borrow and great artists steal. Let us teach you what we've learned from managing thousands of retargeting campaigns so you can get off to a great start.

Getting started with retargeting—or any new marketing technology—can feel overwhelming. Combine the complexities of building a go-to-market strategy and segmentation with the additional variable of creative performance and you may want to call for backup. We're here to take some of that stress away and walk you through the best-in-class creative techniques that we have seen thousands of advertisers succeed with. From winning CTAs, to optimal creative sizes, to how to maximize the creative/landing-page combination, we will show you what works and what to avoid so you can build a great retargeting program from the ground up.

WHAT SIZE SHOULD I START WITH?

According to the IAB, there are 4 universal ad sizes and 12 other sizes that range between rising stars and the infamous other category.[1] In addition, some websites allow unique ad sizes that better fit with the website objectives or publisher revenue goals. We've yet to meet a creative team with endless cycles to resize creative, so getting the most out of what you have is key to making a marketing campaign successful.

---

[1] www.iab.net/guidelines/508676/508767/displayguidelines.

Tip

Start with the big-three ad sizes: 160×600, 728×90, and, most importantly, the 300×250.

Make sure that every retargeting campaign has the three main ad sizes: 300×250, 728×90, and 160×600. You may also hear these ads referred to as a rectangle, leaderboard, and skyscraper, respectively. You'll find that the vast majority of websites use two if not all three of these ad sizes. In most cases, we've found that the 300×250 outperforms the other sizes in terms of click-through conversions, but you want to make sure to employ all three sizes. This will help with brand awareness, click-through conversions, and to help prevent ad blindness.

Average click-through rates (CTR) across all forms of display are: 300×250 is 0.10 percent, 0.12 percent CTR for 728×90, and 0.09 percent CTR for 160×600.

CREATING COMPELLING CREATIVES

Good creative should move people to act. Great creative will inspire people to buy. Great creative combined with the right targeting will build brand advocates and life-long customers. How do you get to great creative? There are a few simple tips you can follow that will get you on your way.

Tip

Use retargeting to test corporate positioning and messaging. See what has the highest click-through rate and use that to build corporate messaging. If done right, this can become a real-time focus group for your business.

1. Keep it simple. As marketers, we love our product (or services). We want to tell the world everything about what makes us great, but when it comes to online advertising, your prospects just don't have that kind of time or attention span. As a marketer you have one to two seconds to capture their attention and your three-sentence positioning statement won't do that. Be succinct and use clear messaging that speaks like a human being, not a marketer.

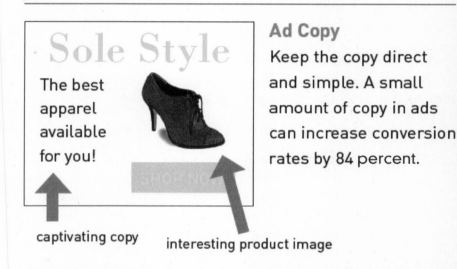

FIGURE 6.1   Sole Style Uses Clear Messaging and a Relevant Image to Drive Interest

2. Clear CTAs. A 300×250 ad doesn't allow for a lot of space to get your message across. We've seen advertisers minimize or even forgo the CTA to err on the side of messaging or a larger logo. Don't fall into this trap. Have a clear, prominent CTA that tells your prospects exactly what action you want them to take. Make sure you test your CTAs because the difference between "Free Demo" and "Watch it in Action" can amount to millions of dollars in revenue for your business.

Call to Action

It's best practice to include a strong call to action. We noticed that including "Shop" in the call to action drove 32 percent higher click-through conversion rates.

strong call to action

FIGURE 6.2   The CTA Is Simple and Prominent

3. Entice and instill urgency. A promotional deadline or mention-limited inventory in your copy will create a sense of scarcity and perceived value. In addition, it will create that deadline that many people need when making a decision. We've seen this work time and again for our retail advertisers.

4. Brand your ads prominently. Use colors and images that complement your brand and ensure your company logo stands out. View-through conversions and view-through traffic increases the more prominent and recognizable your brand is, so make sure your company stands out, even at a quick glance.

5. Be bold! Don't let your ad blend into the website that it is displayed on. Avoid white background and use large, bold typography that stands out and communicates your value proposition. Many websites and ad exchanges require a one-pixel border around ads, so make sure they all have this. You don't want your ads to get rejected by the exchanges.

6. Test, test, test! Test your creative to see what works for your business. Online advertising gives you a massive focus group to test messaging and branding. Use this to your advantage and make sure you test new messaging and CTAs live in market.

7. Rotate creative. One great creative isn't enough. Have multiple creatives and rotate them to prevent ad blindness and determine frequency caps.

COMBATTING AD FATIGUE

In the early days of retargeting, before there were frequency caps and best practices, marketers used to hear a lot of complaints about retargeting that often centered around, "I'm so tired of seeing the same ad everywhere I go." Thankfully, those days are behind us, as retargeting platforms can limit the times a user sees an ad and can also rotate through multiple creatives.

According to Wikipedia, "Banner blindness is a phenomenon in web usability where visitors to a website consciously or subconsciously ignore banner-like information, which can also be called ad blindness or banner noise." Some marketers are trying to combat banner blindness, which is causing a lower response rate and engagement rate, by increasing ad frequency. Unfortunately the increase in volume is now causing ad fatigue, which according to a survey put together by YouGov and Upstream, indicates that 20 percent of U.S. consumers are now less likely to buy a product because of too many ads.[2]

Tip

Ad fatigue happens more quickly when running ads on Facebook versus standard website retargeting because the inventory source is more limited. Rotating creative and messaging is even more important on this channel.

Retargeting, done correctly, not only provides the user with useful information, it can break through banner blindness before fatigue ever sets in. Mona Elesseily, renowned author and VP of Online Marketing for Page Zero Media, has provided us with the following advice for preventing ad fatigue.

---

[2]http://techcrunch.com/2012/02/24/first-look-survey-warns-of-consumers-turning-off-from-digital-ads/.

How to Create Fatigue-Proof Ads
by Mona Elesseily

Use Relevant Keywords and/or Relevant Themes

It's important to ensure you use relevant keyword terms in your ads. If using keyword-based retargeting, consistency between what people are searching for and the keywords that they see in the ads that appear in results are very important. If your retargeting is display based, it's important to use topics/themes that will resonate with your audience and/or fit into your audiences live.

Focus on Customer Benefits

It's not about your company but about the benefits your company provides to its customers. Think about customer benefits and create ads geared to your customer's specific wants. Here are some examples of some possible customer benefits.

- Do people want to be healthier?
- Have more energy?
- Be more efficient at work?

Here are some questions you can answer that will help you uncover the benefits your company provides to customers:

- What's in it for me (customer)?
- What is the end result?
- What are you solving?

For additional insight, conduct focus groups or ask your target audience. Ads that focus on benefits will hold the attention of your audience more.

Try Different Promotions

Use different promotions in your ads and see what works best for the product or service you're selling. Here are some examples: BOGO, buy one and get one 50 percent off, 30 percent off price, 50 percent off price, get 50 percent off your next purchase, and so on. The beauty of retargeting is that marketing messages can change based on visitors' actions on a site. For example, people who've visited a home page can be targeted differently than someone who has abandoned a cart. In the latter example, remarketing messages can target a specific item(s) that were in the abandoned cart. Ads can also be different if they abandon the cart on consecutive occasions.

Try Limited-Time Offers

Limited-time offers create a sense of urgency and encourage people to take action. Here are some examples: "Only for 5 people," "Only for 100 people," and so on. Using the example from above, advertisers who abandoned the cart could see a remarketing ad with a limited-time offer to encourage them to make a purchase quickly.

Include Specific Calls to Action

Include appropriate calls to action in your ads. Here are some examples: click here, act now, try this, start today, visit site, enroll now, and so on. Or maybe your goal is to sell something inexpensive and get repeat business by targeting new customers via e-mail. Whatever it is, know your outcome and gear ads towards those outcomes. The key is to start with clear objective (like e-mail, buy, fan, friend, and so on) and work objectives into specific calls to action.

Use Compelling Images

Images are a very important component of retargeting (if applicable). Images are the number one reason people are attracted to ads (images are attributed 70 to 75 percent of an ad's success). If you are not using images, this makes a good case to try some image-based ads.

These types of images tend to work well:

- Healthy women, happy women, shot from the waist up
- Images with action, involvement, eye contact (women)
- Pictures of animals

(continued)

(continued)
- Pictures that look homely and like you took them yourself
- Logos in images or logo images

Note: Images don't need to tie directly into the product or service you're selling but there should be a logical connection. For example, a company in the health/wellness field can use an image of fruits and vegetables.

Pointer: Step away from computer and see if you can see the image if you're walking by your computer. If not, you'll need to enlarge your image.

Create Strong Headlines

Headlines are important, as they are a good way to grab attention. In pay-per-click (PPC), direct headlines tend to work best but, with remarketing, advertisers can be a little more creative. There are several ways in which one can create powerful and compelling headlines. Here are some examples:

Direct Headline
- Free Cat Food Recipes
- Buy XYZ Today

Indirect Headline
- Plenty of Fish in the Sea
- Take a Load Off

There are news headlines and reason headlines, too. The idea is to be creative and encourage people to be curious.

Easy Changes to Prevent Ad Fatigue

- Add border, corners, and so on.
- Adjust the contrast of the photo (make brighter).
- Change images.

First-Party Data and Creative

As an online marketer, you have access to the most powerful information available about your customers and prospects—your first-party data. You know the pages people visited on your website, how long they spend on the site, the products viewed, and their purchase history. This is more powerful than any information you can buy from a third-party data provider. How does this play a part in your creative strategy? Imagine using your first-party data to customize the ads that someone views. This level of targeting and customization is not only possible, but highly recommended, especially in e-commerce. For instance, the clothing brand, Betabrand considers itself a collection of subbrands that appeal to different audiences. Segmented creatives is key to their retargeting success as they are able to show disco hoodies, one of their most popular clothing items, to a relevant audience and retarget visitors interested in a reversible smoking jacket instead.

How this works:

A visitor goes to www.bustedtees.com to look at clothing. She browses through several items and eventually settles on a brown T-shirt with what resembles a jar of peanut butter on it. After adding the T-shirt to a shopping cart, the visitor gets distracted and abandons the cart and the website. Thanks to retargeting and LiquidAds, Busted Tees can now market to this person with the exact item of clothing she was initially interested in.

FIGURE 6.3 Busted Tees Uses LiquidAds to Show Prospects a Retargeting Ad with This Recently Viewed Product Image

HOW TO SCALE YOUR CREATIVE EFFORTS

Customized creatives across a handful of segments can seem like a lot of work, especially if each creative is manually built, but for e-commerce sites with hundreds or even thousands of items, creative individual ads are nearly impossible. With dynamic ad solutions, like LiquidAds, advertisers can dynamically insert the product that someone viewed in their retargeting ads.

How Udemy Personalized Each Student's Experience with LiquidAds

Udemy, the world's largest destination for on-demand, online courses, empowers over 1,000,000+ members to accelerate their education by recruiting world experts, including *New York Times* best-selling authors, CEOs, and Ivy-League professors to teach everything from programming to yoga.

With hundreds of paid and free courses on topics from gardening to astrophysics, Udemy struggled to quickly scale their advertising in a way that showcases their wide breadth of courses. They solved this challenge with AdRoll's dynamic ad solution, LiquidAds, by creating customized ad experiences for each prospective student.

Within a few days, Udemy could scale their campaigns to serve ads with relevant course recommendations without additional engineering or creative resources. Gokce Cozen, Marketing Manager at Udemy explains," LiquidAds helped us make thousands of personalized ads with no effort. With the dynamic ads, we can include the course name, title, or a discount to drive our users back to our website. LiquidAds gave us an astounding 20 percent average conversion rate in virtually no time."

CREATIVE BEST PRACTICES FOR RETAIL

There are certain best practices that are unique to retail and e-commerce that are worth being discussed independently. If you are in a lead-generation industry, feel free to skip this section of the Creative Best Practices chapter.

As we mentioned earlier in the book, the more targeted your campaign is, the better your results will be. In retail, we've seen significant increases in click-through rates (CTR) when the retargeting creative matches the image that the user has recently viewed. A retail website may have hundreds, thousands, or even tens of thousands of products and no matter how vast a design team may be, creating that many ads by hand just isn't scalable. This is where LiquidAds comes in. As long as your website has a product feed, creating thousands of ads is easy.

Now that you are using dynamic ads, what should you show in them? We've tested three different styles of creative across thousands of retargeting-retail campaigns to determine this. We've tested ads highlighting a product, showcasing a model wearing that product, and focusing on promotions. On average, ads showing a product have a 0.13 percent CTR and average click-to-conversion (CTC) rate of 3.6 percent, which is great. We've seen ads that focus solely on promotion having a lower CTR and CTC at 0.11 percent and 2.38 percent respectively. Promotions have their place, but don't focus all of your creative efforts on them. The best performing ads in the retail space typically highlight a model wearing the recently viewed product. This causes an average 0.18 percent CTR and average 3.7 percent CTC rate.

FIGURE 6.4   In This Ad the Sole Style Model Wearing the Product Viewed Outperforms Other Options

Creative best practices for retargeting on Facebook differ from creative best practices for site retargeting. When retargeting on Facebook, product images actually outperform promotions and models. The product images have a 53 percent higher CTR than benchmark data. So make sure you use the right imagery for each medium. With anything, test what works for your company.

FIGURE 6.5   Be Sure to Test Creative on Facebook as Product Images Tend to Have Higher Performance

BustedTees

BustedTees is one of the web's leading Internet-based T-shirt brands. Started by the guys from collegehumor.com, the founders wanted to make T-shirts that were comical and comfortable. With a wide selection of T-shirts, hoodies, and various other products—all appealing to different audiences—BustedTees knew that using a one-size-fits-all approach to their advertising wouldn't work.

BustedTees used LiquidAds to create a customized advertising experience for each of their website visitors. By using their product feed and dynamically populated ad content, they were able to scale their creative without burdening their marketing team. Using dynamic ads caused an 85 percent increase in conversions and lowered their cost per acquisition (CPA) by 86 percent.

CREATIVE BEST PRACTICES FOR FBX

Retargeting allows you to reengage your website visitors as they browse the web. In September 2012, Facebook opened their platform to allow websites to retarget visitors as they browse Facebook. In spring of 2013, Facebook went a step further and opened retargeting to the News Feed, which has since become one of the most important channels for retargeting. According to the research study, "Facebook Exchange News Feed by the Numbers,"[3] 17 percent of people are only reachable on Facebook, and retargeting in the Facebook newsfeed has a 21× higher CTR than standard web retargeting. We've also found that using Facebook as a key inventory channel as part of larger site retargeting strategy maximizes conversions, sales, and reach for clients.

With the potential for such high click-through rates on Facebook, it is important to look at how to maximize creative performance on the channel.

BASICS OF ADS ON FBX

Ad sizes on Facebook differ from standard ad sizes on the rest of the web. There are two retargeting ad sizes on Facebook: right-hand side ads (launched June 2012) and News Feed page post-link ads (launched May 2013).

Right-Hand Side Ads

Title: Must be under 25 characters. Think short and catchy!
Ad Body: Keep the copy including spaces under 90 characters.
Image Size: 100×72 pixels.
File: Images can be uploaded as .jpg, .gif, or .bmp files.

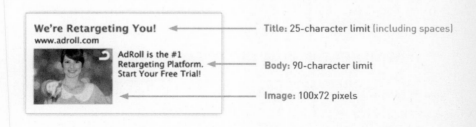

FIGURE 6.6   Basics of a Facebook Right-Hand Side Ad

[3]http://pages.adroll.com/fbx_news_feed_report.html.

News Feed Page Post-Link Ads

Title: Must be under 25 characters. Think short and catchy!
Ad Body: 90-character limit, including spaces.
Image Size: 154×154 pixels (shown as 90×90 pixels for some users).
Post: 500-character limit with the remainder truncated.
File: Images can be uploaded as .jpg, .gif, or .bmp files.

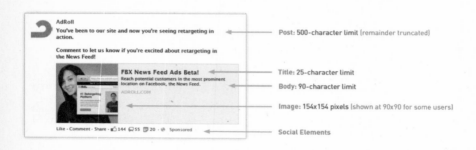

FIGURE 6.7   Anatomy of a Facebook News Feed Ad

FBX AT A GLANCE

Reach: 1 billion active users (June 2012), 57 percent of whom are daily users.
Targeting: Your customer-intent data.
Access: Via FBX Qualified Partners.
Formats: Right-hand side and News Feed on desktop.
Primary Objective: Direct response.

HOW TO GET THE MOST OUT OF FACEBOOK CREATIVES

Now that you know the basic creative types on Facebook, let's talk about how to use them. Right-hand side (RHS) ads typically have a lower click-through rate than News Feed ads. Because of this, to maximize RHS performance, your ads will need to stand out. Vivid use of color, exclamation points, and questions are common best practices. It is also important to keep frequency in mind for Facebook-RHS ads. Depending on the size of your audience and your budget, it is imperative that you rotate right-hand side ads at least every two weeks if not more often.

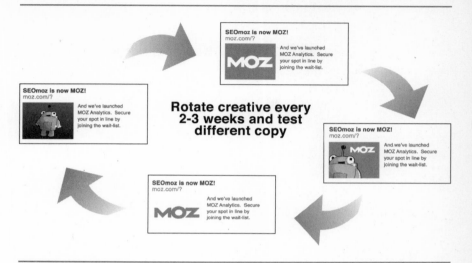

FIGURE 6.8   Moz Does a Great Job of Rotating Creative Every Two Weeks

News Feed ads are the premium placements of the Facebook ecosystem. They take up the most real estate and drive the strongest performance. In fact, according to the report *Facebook Exchange, News Feed by the Numbers*, the average click-through rate of a newsfeed ad is 49× higher than that of a right-hand side ad. To maximize performance of this ad unit, it is important to understand how the ad interacts with a person's News Feed and to know that there is a one impression per person per day frequency cap. This is Facebook's way of not letting people get inundated with ads.

Tips for News Feed Ad Performance

1. Encourage people to like, share, and comment on News Feed ads.
2. Keep your post copy to under 500 characters so it fits easily.

To drive the strongest possible performance on FBX, use dynamic or LiquidAds. A leading retailer, Indochino, had a 102 percent increase in click-through rates once they implemented dynamic ads as part of their Facebook-advertising strategy. To set up LiquidAds, you need to have a product feed. From there, the process is simple.

CHAPTER 7

Advanced Retargeting Strategies

At this point in the book, we are assuming that you have fallen in love with retargeting as much as the authors. The ability to drive bottom-of-the-funnel conversions is one of the most enticing things about this medium. Is there more than targeting shopping cart and form abandoners to drive those quick wins? The answer is yes! Retargeting has so many use cases that go beyond the shopping cart; it can do everything from building brand awareness, to recruiting, to lead nurturing, to fueling holiday growth, and everything in between. Over the course of this chapter, we will walk you through some of the advanced-retargeting strategies that get advertisers more excited than premium-marketing swag.

RETARGETING TO SOLVE FREEMIUM

The freemium model has been around since the 1980s, but it really started to pick up steam in 2006. For those not familiar with the freemium-business model, it's discussed extensively in the book, *Free*, by Chris Anderson. This model is described by Fred Wilson in his blog post, "My Favorite Business Model," as when companies "give [their] service away for free, possibly ad supported but maybe not, acquire a lot of customers very efficiently through word of mouth, referral networks, organic search marketing, and so on, then offer premium priced value added services or an enhanced version of [their] service to [their] customer base."[1] An example of a business with a freemium model is Box, where you get 10 GB of secure storage for free, but if you need more than that you need to pay a monthly fee.

---

[1]www.avc.com/a_vc/2006/03/my_favorite_bus.html.

The problem with the freemium model is converting users from free to paid, as many people get addicted to the free product and don't want to convert to the paid version. Retargeting can help solve the freemium dilemma for many businesses and aid in converting free users to paid ones through a segmented retargeting campaign.

HOW TO USE RETARGETING TO SOLVE THE FREEMIUM DILEMMA

As we mentioned earlier, many people think of retargeting as just a way to get people to fill out a form. At that point, you deploy the burn or conversion code and stop retargeting them. If you are trying to solve the freemium paradox, then your retargeting strategy should begin the moment they sign up for the 14-day free trial or the free version of your product. We are going to walk you through two examples of how to use retargeting to take people through the sales funnel and get them to convert to a paid user.

Let's say you have a product with a 14-day-free trial and you want to get people off that trial as quickly as possible and on to the paid version of your product. Retargeting can help. Once a person completes the free-trial form, rather than removing them from your retargeting program, put him or her into a new segment called Free to Paid. The only way to remove that person from the Free-to-Paid segment is for him or her to enter their credit-card information and ultimately purchase your product. Over the next 14 days, the length of the free trial, use ad sequencing with targeted messaging to move the buyer through the funnel. On the first one to three days rotate welcome messages with upgrade messages. On days four to seven discuss features of the higher edition with an upgrade CTA. On days 8 to 11 discuss the benefits of the higher editions also with an upgrade CTA. On days 12 to 14 have a trial-expiration message. The sense of urgency in these ads should increase over time. If the user hasn't converted after 14 days, spend the next 7 to 14 days with messaging that discusses the trial expiration and benefits of becoming a premium user. Conversion processes will vary by business, so we recommend looking at a conversion histogram to determine at what frequency you should rotate ads and how long this campaign should run for, but this should give you a good starting point.

Nitro Case Study

NitroPDF is the desktop PDF solution of choice for a global-customer base ranging from small businesses to large enterprises. They believe so strongly in the value of their product, that they let prospects use NitroPDF software for free for 14 days. To help move those leads through the sales funnel, they ran a 14-day retargeting campaign with a goal of converting free to paid. Nitro created a segmented program to message trial users throughout each step of the purchasing process to persuade them to buy. By doing this, Nitro Sr. Marketing Manager Sean Zinsmeister explains, "AdRoll [retargeting] has been key in helping us improve that conversion rate."

Freemium models don't always include a free trial, and many businesses give away one user license for free. This is a great way to get mass usage of a product, but getting users from one free license to multiple paid licenses can be a challenge. Retargeting can be an effective way of communicating the value proposition of your product to free users and ultimately get them to buy. If you run a business where someone can use a limited version of your product for free forever then you should look at retargeting as a form of account nurturing. If you are already doing this through e-mail, then you have a great starting point for messaging and length of campaign. Similar to retargeting after a 14-day-free trial, put visitors who have completed the signup form in a custom segment, called "Free to Paid."

To determine how long you should run your campaign, you can start by looking at a histogram that shows your click-through conversions, as shown below. If the majority of your free-to-paid conversions happen within the 11 days, you can focus the majority of your retargeting efforts in that time span. What you will see is that there is a conversion spike around 29 days, so it is worth continuing to engage with free users throughout the course of 30 days, using a 14- to 30-day period, looking to both drive a sense of urgency and show the value of the premium version of your product.

(continued)

(continued)

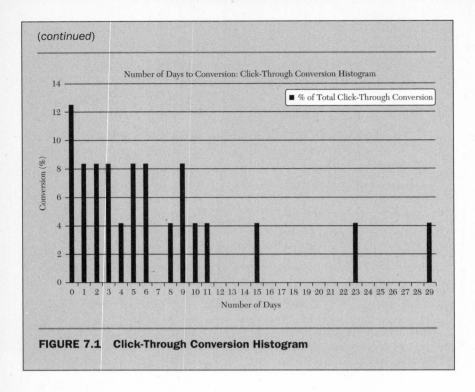

FIGURE 7.1   Click-Through Conversion Histogram

Interview with Matt Sweezey, Pardot and Lauren Vaccarello, AdRoll

In a recent research study on B2B-demand generation, I found that 76 percent of the world's largest software-as-a-service (SaaS) companies use some form of retargeting. Let's equate online ads to e-mail 10 years ago—they're disruptive and don't pull data dynamically from other marketing mediums. However, just like e-mail nurturing gave e-mail new life, I believe combining marketing automation with your retargeting solution will breathe new life into online ads. Once this happens, lead nurturing will no longer be an e-mail-only tactic, but a technique that can help marketers grow relationships over any advertising medium.

The idea is simple. If you can nurture people with e-mail, why can't you do it with ads, too? Until recently, you could only use a single dataset of your website for segmenting your retargeting ads. But what would happen if you could drive your online ads from the same data you currently use to power e-mail-nurturing programs? What happens when you tie marketing automation data and retargeting's reach? To dig deeper into this idea, I connected with Lauren Vaccarello (@LaurenV), the CMO of AdRoll (@AdRoll), to get her thoughts on the concept of digital nurturing.

The big question I wanted to discuss with Lauren was whether or not marketers could nurture people with online ads. Lauren and I explored this topic over a few days, covering both the basics and the advanced nuances of this idea. While the discussion covered some more advanced topics, the concepts are actually pretty simple. What is retargeting used for now? What would happen if you combined it with marketing automation to do digital nurturing? Here are a few of the notes from our conversation.

Mathew Sweezey: How do most people use retargeting currently?

Lauren Vaccarello: A starting point for most companies is to use retargeting as a customer-acquisition tool. It is a great bottom-of-the-funnel tactic to get people who have abandoned shopping carts or forms, and reengage with them so they come back to your website. As marketers, we spend the majority of our time optimizing around the 5 percent who convert immediately. Retargeting lets you market to the 95 percent of people who aren't ready to buy right away and bring them back into your funnel.

MS: What is the typical ROI from just following people with targeted ads?

LV: We have a great customer, Udemy, the largest site for online, on-demand courses, who started with retargeting as a way to drive course sales. Once they combined that with dynamic ads that would show the most recent course someone viewed, their already high ROI increased by 600 percent.

(continued)

(continued)

MS: Can the ads change based on real-time data—the same data that I use to develop my dynamic lead-nurturing programs?

LV: I love this question! Retargeting is all about using customer intent data to build marketing strategies. The way we look at building bidding algorithms and optimizing retargeting is all about using intent signals like pages visited, time on site, purchase history, and recency to make the most out of a campaign. All of these pieces already exist as part of IntentIQ and can be used. What I'm really looking forward to is integrating all of those pieces with other data sources, like e-mail open rates and lead scores, to build a lead-nurturing program that combines e-mail with a corresponding ad campaign. There are some hacks, but we aren't there yet from the standpoint of an out-of-the-box product offering. We are always looking for alpha customers who want to test out some of the new ideas we are developing.[2]

---

[2]www.clickz.com/clickz/column/2290921/lead-nurturing-with-online-ads-the-future-of-retargeting.

RECRUITING, RETARGETING, AND BUILDING YOUR EMPLOYER BRAND

The recruiting team at AdRoll loves retargeting, not just because they believe in the product and the company mission, but also because they see it as a great way of building and extending our employer brand. Setting up an employer/recruiting retargeting campaign is simple. Log into your retargeting platform and create a custom segment around the careers section on your website. If someone hits your main careers page they should go into your general recruiting/employer branding retargeting campaign. Depending on the volume of your website you can also build even more targeted campaigns around recruiting for specific positions. For example, because of AdRoll's focus on technology, hiring engineers is paramount, so we set up a separate retargeting campaign around engineers. If a visitor visits the engineering area of the careers section or visits our tech blog, we retarget them with messaging tied to our values as an employer, our focus on technology, and the fact that we are hiring.

When we opened our office in Dublin in October 2013, we knew we needed to hire fast and the market was competitive, so establishing AdRoll as a compelling place to work was key to us hitting our 2014 hiring target of 100 employees in Dublin. To do this, we used a combination of geotargeting with advanced segmentation. Anyone who visits the careers page and was located in Europe received our recruiting ads. We also incorporated an employer-branding ad into our Irish-retargeting campaigns to help drive awareness that we have a strong local presence but also knowing that the tech community is a tight-knit group and this would help get the word out.

FIGURE 7.2   Recruiting Retargeting Ad

BUILDING COMMUNITY THROUGH RETARGETING

In February 2012, Gartner published a report that indicated the CMO would outspend the CIO within five years and cited technology-based marketing and the rise of Big Data as fuel to this trend.[3] At the same time,

---

[3]www.forbes.com/sites/lisaarthur/2012/02/08/five-years-from-now-cmos-will-spend-more-on-it-than-cios-do/.

there has been an increasing number of articles discussing how marketing is changing, which in many ways is focused on the evolution of the customer and the overall customer journey. Marketing is no longer just about a one-and-done, direct-sales approach, but is increasingly about the long-term customer relationship.

With that in mind, we started to look at ways retargeting can help build strong relationships with customers and instill a sense of community. For this, your retargeting programs will start not at the shopping cart or product page, but at your thank you or confirmation page. Once someone purchases your product, rather than removing them from all retargeting programs, you can instead put them into a loyalty campaign or go even further and put them into a community campaign.

If your company already has an established community, for the week-after-purchase message let the buyer know you have a community and encourage them to join. Encourage buyers to share their stories. Facebook News Feed ads are a great vehicle for this as they are inherently social and encourage interaction. For example, AdRoll encourages people to comment and post on their ads on Facebook. Not only does this allow for candid conversations, but it also causes a nice viral effect as the post now appears to the commenter's friends.

FIGURE 7.3   Facebook News Feed Ad Encouraging Comments

Betabrand Seamlessly Builds Their Community

Instead of worrying about whether auburn is in this season or developing a cohesive line for the fashion critics, Betabrand focuses on creating clothing based directly on their community's feedback. Each week, the company releases a new item in limited batches depending on their customer's previous votes and comments during the conception process. From their clever, Bike-to-Work pants (bike-to-boardroom ready, reflective, khaki pants) to their reversible disco hoodies, the San Francisco-based retailer has created a cult-like following of Betabrand fanatics eager to wear something contrary to the fashion norm.

Since Betabrand creates whimsical, yet functional, clothing based on their community's tastes, they use LiquidAds on Facebook Exchange to crowdsource design ideas for future products. When Betabrand wanted to grow their existing community, they leaned on LiquidAds to promote their customer-model contest, Model Citizen.

FIGURE 7.4   Betabrands Use LiquidAds to Promote Their Model Citizen Program

By showcasing ads of customers wearing their signature smoking jackets or limited edition Panther Suits, Betabrand reengaged previous purchasers on Facebook and encouraged them to model in their favorite Betabrand garb. Betabrand models were also able to promote their photos to their friends who were then targeted with ads encouraging them to become Model Citizens as well. With thousands of customer-model photos submitted and a weekly flow of new customer-generated products, LiquidAds made it simple to create custom

(*continued*)

(*continued*)
ads at scale and drive engagement without additional resources or work from Betabrand's marketing team. "I'm spending less of my time in the hands-on muck of dealing with campaigns" says Matt Thier, Cofounder of Betabrand, "Instead, I have more time to focus on initiatives that will drive additional value to me and the company. It gives me more bandwidth."

USING RETARGETING TO DRIVE AWARENESS

Retargeting is often viewed as just a bottom-of-the-funnel tactic. What many marketers don't always see is that retargeting is a great way to increase awareness and reach as it can make you look bigger than you are.

Let's face it, marketers don't have enough budget. It doesn't matter if you work at a 3-person company or a 30,000-person company, budgets are always tight and you wish you had more money to accomplish your goals. For small to medium-sized businesses and for startups, looking bigger than you are is key to competing with larger companies. Retargeting allows you to do just that.

Retargeting and the Big Game

Several years ago, I (Lauren) worked on a product launch for Chatter.com, Salesforce.com's corporate collaboration product. Salesforce.com really believed in the product and in the idea that the way businesses are working is changing and that increased collaboration between employees, employees and customers, and customers and products was at the crux of that change. To make a big splash with the product, Salesforce launched a Super Bowl ad. Budgets were massive and there was a lot of time spent on having that one big splash and driving as much traffic to Chatter.com as possible. As the online marketer in the group, I wanted to extend the reach of the Super Bowl ad digitally. I knew ad campaigns of this scale drive a burst of traffic, but I wondered how to both convert that traffic and how to provided sustained awareness on those initially exposed to the television ad, as it takes 7 to 10 marketing touches before brand recognition starts to take place. Enter retargeting. We placed retargeting tags on Chatter.com and prepped for the influx of traffic. We also created a series of ads that would educate people on what the product did to drive further awareness and ultimately lead to more conversions.

As expected, February 6th hit and the Super Bowl drew over 100 million viewers, and Salesforce.com's two commercials—a 30-second spot before the halftime show and a 15-second spot after—got a lot of views and drove significant web traffic and conversions. Over 30 days after the Super Bowl, we continued to retarget those website visitors with Chatter creative. The comparatively small investment in retargeting nearly doubled the amount of conversions from the Super Bowl, and increased brand awareness among the millions of people who otherwise would have been exposed to the product only one time.

HOLIDAY RETARGETING STRATEGIES

With site traffic tripling, the holiday season is the most important time of year for many online retailers. According to today.com, 6 out of 10 online retailers start their holiday promotions before Halloween.[4] Maximizing returns during this short two- to three-month time frame can literally make or break some businesses. To put how important the holiday season is into perspective, there was over $42 billion spent in 2012, which was up 14 percent from the prior year.[5] Now that you know why nailing the holiday shopping season is so important, let's talk about how you can use retargeting to maximize returns.

FIGURE 7.5   Holiday Facts

Sources: [1]http://www.today.com/money/happy-halloween-now-lets-talk-holiday-shopping-1C677 9077; [2]http://www.comscore.com/Insights/Press_Releases/2013/1/2012_U.S._Online_Holiday_Spend ing_Grows_14_Percent_vs_Year_Ago_to_42.3_Billion; [3]Prosper Insights & Analytics/Shop.org Post-Holiday Consumer Study, Dec. 27, 2012 to Jan. 9, 2013. 2013.

[4]www.today.com/money/happy-halloween-now-lets-talk-holiday-shopping-1C6779077.

[5]www.comscore.com/Insights/Press_Releases/2013/1/2012_U.S._Online_Holiday_Spending_Grows_14_Percent_vs_Year_Ago_to_42.3_Billion.

Prepare for Increased Competition

The holiday season is peak season for online advertisers. Keep in mind, everyone is aggressively trying to stay in front of their customers, so it's important to increase your cost-per-mille (CPM) bid. This gives you a greater chance of reaching shoppers during the busiest time of the year! In addition to increasing your CPM bid, you might want to consider increasing the frequency with which you are showing your ads. Competitors will likely be making a strong holiday push. Make sure that you stand out by being in front of your visitors as often as possible, as the last thing you want to miss out on is valuable sales opportunities.

Use Holiday Creatives to Promote Holiday Deals

Oftentimes advertisers think it's enough to simply ramp up their budgets to drive holiday shoppers to their website. However, you'll see higher ROI by putting together some holiday-specific creative that clearly shows any promotions you may be offering or seasonal merchandise you may be selling. With 39.7 percent of holiday shoppers seeking free shipping and 20.9 percent comparing prices online, holiday shoppers are on the lookout for deals. Give them themed creative and deals for those holiday presents!

Target Past Purchasers

Your most likely customers are often people who have purchased your products in the past. According to a Shop.Org survey of 2011 holiday shoppers, 63 percent of shoppers had previously shopped on the website before and returned during the holiday season to shop for gifts. Who better to target with holiday advertising than your current customers? If they own a product of yours that they love, they are more likely to purchase it as a present for their friends and family. It's common to remove recent customers from your retargeting campaign but during the holidays customers often make multiple purchases within a short time period, so make sure to stay top of mind with this audience.

A great way to target past purchasers is with CRM retargeting. CRM retargeting enables brands to leverage their valuable CRM and offline data to reach potential customers who haven't visited their site across the web and Facebook. Holiday retailers can use the customer information that has been gathered over the past few seasons to reengage shoppers before they visitor your site.

Expand Your Cookie Pool

Throughout the year, it's common to target users who have been to your site in the past 30 or 90 days. During the holidays, it's a good idea to look beyond your most recent users and target people who last visited your site further in the past in order to reengage their interest. It's fair game to assume that they'll return to buy that exact same item or others as gifts for the holidays.

Think about the Customer Journey

When planning out creative, think about how to influence the buyer beyond just that first impression. Set up a multistage campaign with sequential and escalating offers to guide potential customers through the purchase funnel.

Reengage across All Platforms

Don't limit yourself to just one inventory source. Make sure your retargeting efforts expand across the open web on exchanges like Google's AdX, Yahoo!, Appnexus, and AOL, as well as social networks like Facebook's FBX. When on FBX, make sure your ads appear on both Facebook's News Feed and on the right-hand side through Facebook Exchange (FBX).

KEEP THE LIGHTS ON AFTER THE HOLIDAYS

Though the shopping frenzy fades following Christmas, shoppers are still on the hunt for great deals, especially after receiving cash and gift cards over the holidays. It's not the time to go dark. After the peak holiday shopping period, we traditionally see prices plummet 25 percent. Once the holiday season ends, refresh your creatives and try to entice gift-card holders and post-holiday buyers.

New Years
CPMs
December
January

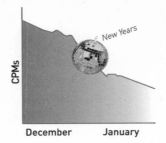

FIGURE 7.6 Holiday CPMs

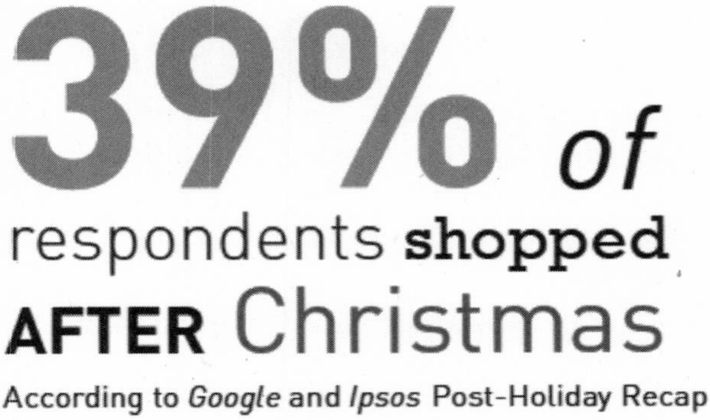

39% of
respondents shopped
AFTER Christmas
According to Google and Ipsos Post-Holiday Recap

FIGURE 7.7 Post-Holiday Sales

Source: "Post Holiday Learnings for 2012," Google, www.google.com/think/research-studies/post-holiday-learnings-for-2012.html.

Ruche

Ruche is a modern boutique with a vintage-inspired touch. Founded in May 2005, Ruche strives to support small boutique brands and indie designers. As the holiday season approached, Ruche sought to re-engage their customers and inform them about their holiday promotions. Partnering with AdRoll allowed Ruche to target website visitors throughout the shopping funnel with holiday-specific ads. The ads were designed to lead website visitors to Ruche's holiday-themed website. Since the company was focused on increasing sales during this competitive period, attention was focused on optimizing campaigns by pausing under-performing ads, adjusting segmentation, and changing cookie durations to suit the holiday rush. Sean Switzer, Director of Advertising at Ruche, notes, "The holiday season is one of the most important times for an e-commerce site, and we were focused on maximizing our conversions. Overall, we've always had strong performance with our retargeting campaigns; however, during the holiday season, the AdRoll optimizations led to our click-through rates increasing by 42 percent and our retargeting ROI increasing by 17 percent."

GEOTARGETING TO DRIVE IN-STORE SALES

Many online retailers also have brick-and-mortar stores or sell through partners' shops. Retargeting is a great tactic to help drive online sales, but can it also be used to drive in-store purchases? The answer to that question is yes. For many online products, in particular high-end goods, the in-store experience is important to closing sales. We looked at this paradox of using online to drive offline and worked with dozens of retail customers to come up with a plan that would help maximize revenue for the business, not just the e-commerce side of the house. To make this strategy work, you must use geotargeting.

We'll walk you through an example. Let's say you have five brick-and-mortar stores throughout the United States. One in Manhattan, in 10023, one in San Francisco in 94108, one in Chicago in 60601, one in Los Angeles in 90036, and one in Boston in 02115. Determine the radius of each store in which locals visit. In Manhattan the shopping radius may be smaller than in Los Angeles. For the sake of this example, we will say that shoppers within 30 miles are likely to visit the store. In your retargeting platform, create custom segments for geo and change your creatives. Now, if someone from NYC 10028 visits your website, rather than only retargeting them with creative sending them back to your website, you provide alternate messaging that directs them to a new store or to the store-locator page. To track performance, try using a *reserve-in-store* option. This will allow shoppers to pick out a product or products online and go to the store to see it in person. If this isn't possible, you can use visiting the store-locator page as a microconversion.

As online marketers we want to track and measure everything, but with driving online browsing to in-store sales, there will be some gray areas. Ultimately you want to drive revenue for the business, so keep an eye on how store sales are going once your retargeting program starts to promote visiting local shops.

CONCLUSION

Retargeting has many use cases beyond just converting bottom-of-the-funnel website visitors. It is important to think about your business goals and how retargeting can help you achieve them. Whether the holidays are coming up and you want to maximize revenue or you need to speed up close rates on complex sales, retargeting can play a role.

CHAPTER 8

Introduction to Measurement and Attribution

Attribution has become a hot topic in the marketing world with heated debates over first-touch, last-touch, and multitouch attribution methods. Unfortunately, there is no clear right or wrong way to do attribution that will work for everyone. When thinking about how to properly measure your retargeting campaign, or any marketing campaign for that matter, you should decide on the objective of that campaign and have a system in place for measuring to see if you accomplish that objective. It sounds simple and obvious, but sometimes marketers launch into using a new technology or marketing tactic without clearly defining what they're trying to accomplish and how they'll decide if they accomplished what they set out to.

It's actually not surprising that this step is sometimes missed since setting clear objectives can actually be a bit complicated. However, when you boil it down to how you're going to measure success, you realize how important it is to define your objectives. Let's look at a few good and bad examples to help articulate this.

A BAD OR VAGUE MARKETING OBJECTIVE: INCREASE SALES

Of course every business wants to increase their sales, but what does that really mean? Does that mean finding new customers? Does it mean increasing loyalty and repeat purchases? Does it mean launching a new product? Could it even mean increasing your prices? That would certainly result in larger sales by certain measures even if it resulted in fewer customers. So let's look at ways to refine this objective to make it more specific and measurable.

A GOOD MARKETING OBJECTIVE: INCREASE SALES BY IMPROVING CUSTOMER-LIFETIME VALUE (LTV) AND RETENTION

By clarifying the true business objective and making it more specific, we can now apply clear metrics that will allow us to evaluate performance. We'll know what segment of customers to look at, and we'll be able to compare a customer's lifetime value (LTV) over a certain period, (for example, the first 90 days of being a customer) from before we launched the campaign compared to after the campaign launched. If the increase in LTV is more than the cost of the marketing campaign, we know we achieved positive ROI. Understanding that improving customer-lifetime value is the ultimate goal will also allow your marketing team to better focus their efforts that drive LTV.

Baseline Customer 90-day Spend	$100
Post-Campaign 90-day Spend	$125
Increase/Decrease in 90-day LTV	$25
Total Customers Exposed	1,000
Incremental Spend	$25,000
Cost of Marketing Campaign	$10,000
ROI	2.5

FIGURE 8.1   Look at Total Customer Value to Determine ROI

LAST-CLICK ATTRIBUTION AND ITS PITFALLS

Last-click attribution is a way of measuring marketing performance in which all of the credit for marketing success is given to whatever drove the last click before a conversion takes place. This model often over-weighs things, like branded search or e-mail, and discounts all of the channels that led to that final action.

Last-click attribution can be a fairly straightforward example, but let's look at how this can get a bit more complicated.

Here's a seemingly simple marketing objective for a hypothetical online-apparel retailer: acquire new first-time customers. For this objective you'd probably want to measure the cost per acquisition (CPA) and probably also the average-order value to make sure you're finding high-quality customers, and not people who behave differently from what you'd expect, such as those who just buy the cheapest item.

Let's look at a diagram of a customer's exposure to a brand over time that shows all the various marketing touch points.

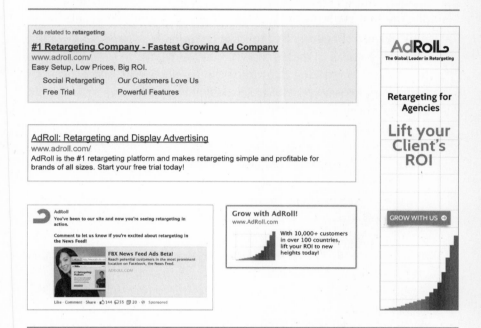

FIGURE 8.2   Diagram of a Series of Interactions a Prospect May Have with Your Brand before Converting

According to a report by Google Analytics, customers interact with a brand 4.3 times over a two-day period before making a purchase.[1] So, which touchpoint should get credit for driving the sale? Looking at the example above, would it be the prospect's first exposure on Facebook? How about the first time the person clicked on an ad bringing them to the site? Certainly that was crucial in driving the eventual sales. Unfortunately, in the last-click attribution model, the only thing that is considered is what drove that final click immediately prior to the purchase.

---

[1]http://analytics.blogspot.com/2012/05/looking-ahead-at-next-generation.html.

Let's examine some potential flaws in the model of last-click attribution:

1. If you give all of the credit to the marketing channel that drives the final interaction, you'll ignore all of the top-of-the-funnel marketing tactics that create awareness in the first place. This can cause budgets and efforts to be overweight to just bottom-of-the-funnel marketing tactics. Over time, this will have a negative impact on your business because if you're not creating awareness, there won't be any last clicks to measure.

2. In addition to ignoring the top-of-the-funnel levers, last-click attribution also causes you to disregard all of the marketing touches that assist in bringing the customer through the consideration process. As we discussed in Chapter 1, it is important to look at the entire funnel, as it takes multiple marketing touches to move people from awareness, to consideration, and ultimately to close. The days of the Apple 1984 commercial—where one compelling Super Bowl ad built a business—are gone, and it is becoming increasingly rare that people can be exposed to a brand once and are immediately won over. Your prospects need to be presented with a brand multiple times to instill a sense of trust, to be reminded of various value propositions, and sometimes to even be won over with promotions.

3. Beyond just underweighting the rest of the marketing funnel, last-click attribution also ignores any marketing touch point anywhere in the customer lifecycle that isn't associated with a click. As we know from decades of traditional (offline) marketing, clicks aren't the only form of exposure to advertising that generates results. There is no click in a TV ad, yet they've proven to be a major driver of awareness, brand perception, customer loyalty, and even direct response. The value of an ad that is viewed at the right time for the right audience is completely discounted and, again, branded search becomes overweight. Last-click attribution doesn't take into account what actually caused that person to search for your product or services online.

Although the attribution landscape is changing rapidly and technology is advancing to better understand the full marketing funnel, last-click attribution is still widely used despite most marketers understanding its various weaknesses.

CONVERSION TYPES: CLICK-THROUGH VERSUS VIEW-THROUGH CONVERSIONS

One of the key debates that invariably come up when discussing attribution relates to click-through and view-through conversions. A click-through conversion occurs when a marketing activity encourages a person to click on an advertisement and eventually converts. A view-through conversion is different, as it occurs when a person views an advertisement, but doesn't click, then eventually converts.

One key thing to keep in mind when attributing credit for a conversion to a particular marketing activity (whether it be click through or view through) is the *look-back window*.

Contrary to what some might expect based on the term, a click-through conversion does not necessarily mean that someone clicks on an ad and immediately goes to a website and purchases. For example, if a brand is running a paid-search campaign that results in a person clicking to their website, but that person doesn't convert until a year later, should that paid-search ad still get credit for the conversion? Certainly as time goes by, the role that ad had in the person buying becomes less and less of an important factor.

Similarly, expecting that an ad campaign will result in a person clicking and immediately flying through the order experience in the same session is a very high bar that wouldn't give credit to perfectly effective advertising campaigns that drive high-quality traffic. However, user-web behavior usually involves multiple visits to a site over a period of time before a conversion takes place, so not taking this into account would result in inaccurately valuing advertising activities.

That's where the look-back window comes into play. In simple terms, the look-back window is the time between which a person is exposed to a marketing activity and then actually completes the desired action, that is, convert.

The industry standard for click conversions is usually 30 days. That's the default measurement in Google Analytics, which is the most widely used attribution system. However, 30 days is not written in stone. With view-through conversions, in particular, many marketers prefer to shorten the look-back window so they only count a view-through conversion if someone sees an ad and then converts within seven days, or even sometimes 24 hours.

Different businesses have different requirements when it comes to attributing conversions. Some want to be more aggressive in their marketing, and therefore err on the side of giving more credit to an advertising channel that eventually leads to a conversion. Some might be more conservative and tighten up the requirements at the risk of undervaluing some of their activities. Let's look at some of these various options in the next section.

ALTERNATIVES TO LAST-CLICK ATTRIBUTION

When looking at a holistic-marketing strategy that includes multiple customer-touch points, the ideal attribution model would look at the entire customer path and give credit to all of the various touches. This is often referred to as *multi-touch attribution* since you're taking into account more than just the last touch. Multi-touch attribution models can be more or less sophisticated, but the goal is always to ensure you're properly rewarding all of your marketing channels, and not just the one that's driving the last action.

One simple version of a multi-touch attribution model would be one that gives a specific, static percentage of the total conversion to the first touch (or initiator), another percentage for the last click, and then split the remaining amount to the assists that happen throughout the customer journey. This model might look something like this:

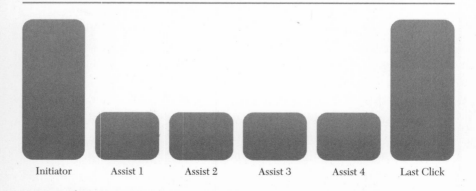

| Initiator | Assist 1 | Assist 2 | Assist 3 | Assist 4 | Last Click |

FIGURE 8.3   Multi-Touch Attribution across Six Touch Points

Another example of multi-touch attribution is a waterfall approach that credits conversions differently based on click versus view and during which look-back window it took place in. The idea is you can determine how impactful the ad impression was based on these factors. Here's an example of how this is set up:

Conversion Type	Attribution %	Number of Conversions	Conversion Values	Attributed Revenue
Click through	100%	25	$350.00	$350.00
<24-hour view through	50%	100	$1,400.00	$700.00
1–7 day view through	25%	150	$2,100.00	$525.00
7–14 day view through	10%	200	$2,800.00	$280.00
			Total Attributed Revenue	$1,855.00
			Media Spend	$900.00
			ROI	2.1×

As you can see in the chart, conversions of different types get different amounts of credit. The final column is the product of the value of the conversions that occurred multiplied by the percent attribution in the second column. If you sum the far right column, you get the total attributed revenue which you can compare to the media spend required to generate that revenue to determine your ROI. In this example, an ROI of 2.1× means that this campaign generated $2.10 in attributed revenue for every $1 in media spend. That's pretty strong positive ROI.

Sophisticated marketers, who have lots or marketing and conversion data to work with, use even more complicated attribution models based on statistical regressions. Basically, using statistics, they can look at all of their conversions during a certain period and all of the customer paths that led to those conversions. They can then see how each marketing channel influences the likelihood of a conversion and can then weight that channel accordingly in their attribution model.

HOW INCREMENTALITY IMPACTS RETARGETING

It's hard to say that one attribution model is the right one. Each marketer has their own set of concerns and challenges, so vendors need to maintain room for flexibility. However, site retargeting is one of the few marketing channels where it's actually quite straightforward to measure incremental lift, and too few marketers take advantage of this.

There's been plenty written about the weaknesses of last-click attribution models, so we'll just touch on the topic briefly. With retargeting in particular, it's dangerous to focus on last-click attribution models since you're only targeting people who've already been to your site. Many of these site visitors would return on their own if you did nothing, so measuring retargeting solely on clicks means you're definitely paying for site visitors who would have come back on their own for free.

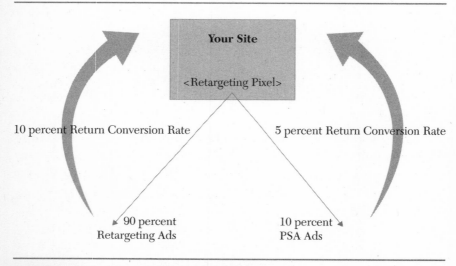

FIGURE 8.4   How Incrementality Works

To properly account for this, advertisers can use a hold-out control group to measure lift. This is a population of randomly selected visitors to an advertiser's site who are not shown retargeting ads (ideally, they're shown control PSA ads). This group can be compared to the behavior of a default group that does see the advertiser's retargeting ads. It's then fairly straightforward to measure the incremental-conversion rate between the group that gets retargeted compared to the group that doesn't. This ensures that you're only measuring the true lift that retargeting delivers, and not counting customers (whether for clicks, views, engagements, and so on) who would have returned to your site on their own.

FIGURE 8.5 Here You Can See the Main Ad and PSA Ad Used to Check for Incrementality

For this type of A/B test, the optimization techniques that drive more incremental conversions versus lower cost per clicks (CPCs) and last-click cost per action (CPAs) are quite different. Here are some tactics that focus on generating lift over shifting credit from other (possibly free) marketing channels.

TIME COHORTS

Perhaps the most underutilized optimization lever within a retargeting campaign is based on time cohorts. We've found that for many advertisers, if they did no retargeting whatsoever, 80 to 90 percent of conversions would occur within five days of a person's first visit to the site. If the focus were to simply drive the lowest last-click CPA, it would be ideal to include retargeting efforts during this time period in the results in order to get credit for as many conversions as possible. However, this would probably be taking credit for a large number of conversions that would've happened anyway. If we're optimizing for incremental lift, we have to explore other time cohorts and techniques to re-engage dormant users and ensure that retargeting generates enough incremental conversions to justify the media spend.

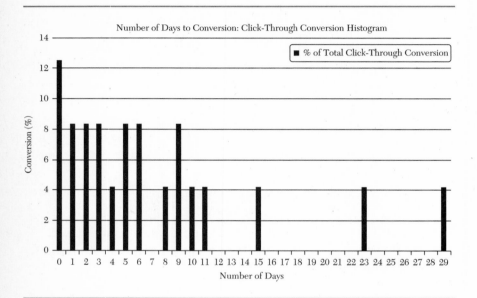

FIGURE 8.6   Time Cohorts

ON-SITE BEHAVIORAL PATTERNS

Who are the most likely visitors to click on an ad and convert once they've left your site? The shopping cart is probably the best place to start. When trying to optimize for the lowest CPC and lowest last-click CPA, focusing on the people who put items in their cart is the lowest-hanging fruit. However, aren't these people also the most likely to come back and convert on their own? When optimizing for incremental lift instead of cheap clicks, retargeting vendors have to explore other intent signals and other areas of a site that might signal high-potential customers. This could include specific products for an online merchant or a specific feature page for a B2B company.

CREATIVE DESIGNED FOR LIFT, NOT CLICKS

If you want to generate lift and incremental conversions, you need to inspire desire in consumers who are on the fence. It's amazing how much this basic principle of advertising is forgotten when we strap our direct-response hats on too tightly. Lift-oriented creative requires attractively designed units that reinforce a value proposition and feature the best possible product imagery and branding. On the other hand, if clicks and a low CPC are the only goal, something that looks more like a shopping widget might make more sense. You'll want to maximize interest by showing a variety of products. Chapter 7 also discussed quite a few best practices for creative. It is important to think about the entire marketing funnel when designing your ads and to understand the goal of each ad.

FREQUENCY CAPS

Retargeting often gets a bad rap for showing too many of the same or similar ads to website visitors. Using multiple vendors for the same cookie pool is often a culprit. However, this problem can be exacerbated by the attribution model. If a retargeting vendor is getting compensated and measured by clicks, it's only natural that they err on the side of being in front of a user more times in order to get that click. If incremental lift is the goal, the vendor needs to tread more carefully. A lift-oriented strategy will focus more closely on the average number of impressions prior to conversion and prioritize exposure during that period, while tapering off after the point of diminishing returns.

Brands and their agencies have a variety of reasons for why they attribute different channels in different ways. However, with site retargeting, you can clearly measure the incremental lift it delivers, so why not take advantage of these techniques to optimize lift?

CONCLUSION

Measuring your retargeting campaigns, and your marketing campaigns in general, can be tricky as the attribution landscape is still being paved.

The first step to truly measuring the success of this program is to understand what your goals are and be concrete. Once you know what you are looking to measure, then look at the entire marketing picture and understand how each touch impacts the sales cycle. Finally, although no marketing attribution model is perfect, it is important to choose one and stick with it.

CHAPTER 9

Business Model Evolution

As discussed in Chapter 2, digital-media buying evolved from being centered on single-publisher buys, to ad networks that aggregated many publishers, to real-time exchanges that auction each ad impression within 50 milliseconds to the highest bidder.

This evolution has not been black and white. Various models still exist and advertisers today might use direct-publisher buys in combination with ad networks, as well as various exchange-based technologies, depending on their goals.

One of the key aspects for understanding the various options is to understand how the companies that offer them make money. Obviously this is important to understand since using a vendor will impact your overall costs, but a vendor's business model also provides useful insight into how they're incentivized to behave. For example, if a vendor's pricing model is based on charging for clicks, they're incentivized to deliver clicks at all costs. What implications might that have? How might that incentive complement your goals and how might it come into conflict? These are the tradeoffs we will review in this chapter.

BUSINESS MODEL OVERVIEW

There are essentially two main types of business models in the media buying ecosystem: transparent and arbitrage. With transparent pricing models, the vendor either charges based on the actual media spend executed through their system or by charging a flat fee that could be monthly, quarterly, or annually depending on how the agreement is negotiated. In any case, these models are referred to as *transparent* because the actual cost of the media is exposed.

When pricing is based on actual media spend, it is often referred to as dynamic CPM, or dCPM. In this case the vendor bids in auctions on various exchanges on behalf of an advertiser. The actual clearing price for each impression varies depending on the dynamics of the auction. The vendor then applies a mark-up percentage on top of the actual cost determined by the auction, and that dictates the price for the end advertiser. For example, if the actual winning bid for an impression is $1 CPM and the vendor charges 35 percent, the cost to the advertiser will be $1.35 CPM.

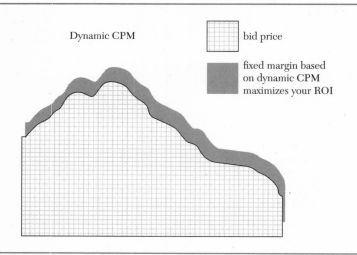

FIGURE 9.1   How dCPMs Work

In transparent pricing models, the vendor usually shares data for all aspects of the campaign: performance by campaign, segment, ad creative, and even detailed visibility into the actual sites the campaign ran on.

In an arbitrage-based pricing model, the vendor buys media on exchanges, ad networks, and/or directly from publishers on a dCPM basis and charges the advertiser based on some other pricing mode, like CPC or CPA. This allows the vendor to make a margin based on what the actual CPC or CPA is based on, the actual inventory cost, and the CPC or CPA they end up charging the advertiser. For example, let's say a vendor buys 100,000 impressions and the actual aggregate dCPM of the auctions for those impressions is $1.50. That means the actual cost of the media is $150. Let's assume this media buy generates a 0.20 percent CTR, resulting in 200 clicks (0.20 × 100,000), so the actual CPC for this campaign is $0.75. However, in order to ensure they make a margin, the vendor will negotiate a CPC that they know will be in excess of the actual CPC of the campaign, let's say $1.40. In that case, the advertiser will pay a $1.40 CPC but the actual CPC will be $0.75, so the vendor will make $0.65 for each click, or a 46 percent margin.

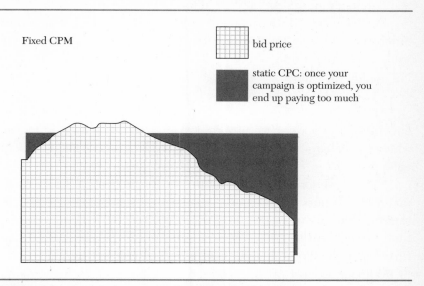

Fixed CPM

bid price

static CPC: once your campaign is optimized, you end up paying too much

FIGURE 9.2   Understanding Pricing Arbitrage

In arbitrage-based pricing models, the advertiser gets less visibility into the detailed metrics of the campaign. Since the vendor is making their margin based on taking the risk of buying inventory, they retain these insights instead of sharing them with the end advertiser.

HOW PRICING MODELS DRIVE VENDOR INCENTIVES

When executing performance marketing campaigns, there is a simple equation that must be solved. You need: media spend, a margin that reflects the value created by a technology provider and the resulting return on investment (ROI), which needs to exceed the advertiser's goals.

Media costs + vendor costs < target acquisition cost (ROI)

Unfortunately, a disproportionate amount of time is spent focused on the left side of the equation, rather than trying to make the right side—the ROI—higher.

Pricing model and negotiating the vendor margin can influence the left side. The right side can be influenced by more strategic and durable factors, such as campaign strategy, optimization plan, creative, and core technology like bidding algorithms.

Focusing on the right side, or ROI, frees up attribution to take a more prominent role in the execution, since it decouples pricing model from measuring results. When I ask marketers why they care about pricing model, they often say that performance-based pricing, such as CPA or CPC, aligns the vendor with their goals.

This can be a dangerous misconception. All these models do is encourage the vendor to optimize around an attribution model upon which they charge and control. Pricing model doesn't change the original equation.

Will the vendor continue running a campaign if they don't make a margin? Of course not—they'll call back to renegotiate pricing if the arbitrage doesn't work out. Will the marketer use vendor reporting as the source of truth? Not a chance—they'll use reporting from their ad server or, hopefully, a neutral third-party analytics solution.

Who cares what pricing model the vendor employs if the marketer isn't going to use the vendor's reporting as the source of truth? Regardless of the pricing model, there is a cost that must be justified based on the marketer's target ROI, which is measured in an entirely different system. Focusing on the pricing model takes away from focusing on achieving and measuring actual results.

Please note: I'm not suggesting that ad-tech vendors be held unaccountable in contractual terms. However, if an advertiser wants to negotiate a term that aligns the vendor with their goals, instead of pricing model or margin, I recommend pushing on lowering the minimum spend amount. If a customer can leave at any time, that's the sure way to align the vendor to deliver results on the customer's terms, based on the attribution model of their choosing.

For example, sometimes a marketer will want to change campaign variables that actually lower performance, such as adjusting frequency caps, running a seasonal flight, or excluding publishers. If the vendor is only rewarded for clicks or conversions, they don't have an incentive to be flexible on those points. Now if the pricing model is based on actual media spending, and the advertiser can pull out any time, will the vendor accommodate those and other requests? Absolutely.

Focusing on vendor margin, just like focusing on margin when buying any product, isn't a good way to assure quality. It's quite the opposite. Diageo makes a larger margin on Ketel One than on Smirnoff, but that doesn't mean you'd rather have Smirnoff in your martini.

Look at the recent succession of ad-tech IPOs. Are the 40 percent-plus margins demanded by companies like Rocket Fuel and Criteo unreasonable? Not if those margins are indicative of the value those companies bring their customers.

PROGRAMMATIC PREMIUM

One of the most notable recent trends in the exchange ecosystem is the rise of a concept called *programmatic premium*. Historically, premium inventory—that is, the first impression on the home page—featured above-the-fold placements, and early impressions in the user journey across the site were reserved by top publishers for their own internal ad sales team to sell directly to advertisers.

FIGURE 9.3 Ad Space above the Line Is Considered above the Fold and below the Line Is Considered below the Fold

The rationale was that these high-value placements demand a higher CPM and required custom treatment by the publisher to properly send traffic to them. They are also often sold on a guaranteed basis. While exchanges have huge amounts of volume, impressions are sold on an auction basis, so technically, delivery isn't guaranteed.

In certain cases, this guarantee can be very important for a brand or agency trying to plan their media spends. For example, Citibank might require that a certain amount of their media spend be on finance-oriented publications. In that situation, Citibank's agency would want to allocate some of the budget to premium direct buys on sites like the *Wall Street Journal* and the finance section of the *New York Times*.

Once a publisher sold as much premium inventory as they could directly, they would historically make any unsold impressions available on exchanges. For that reason, exchange inventory has developed the reputation for being remnant or the unsold portions of various publishers' ad inventory.

Direct buys have historically been negotiated over the phone or e-mail, contracted by a paper insertion order that gets faxed back and forth, manually trafficked by an ad operations person, and measured as a one-off through the advertiser's ad server.

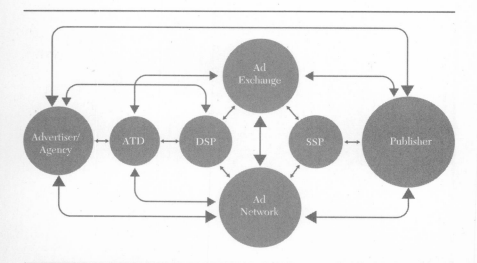

FIGURE 9.4   How a Supply-Side Platform Works

However, this practice is starting to change. Exchanges and supply-side platforms (SSPs) are starting to build in functionality that makes it easier for top publishers to sell their premium inventory via real-time bidding. For example, instead of just putting all impressions into the exchange for the highest bidder, exchanges are making it possible for publishers to set pricing floors for certain sets of premium inventory. The logic being that as long as a minimum price is met, an ad sales team doesn't have to negotiate individual deals and traffic one-off campaigns. Instead, publishers can segment premium inventory, make buyers aware that it's premium, then leverage the highly efficient auction environment and exchange buying to execute the campaign.

In addition to price floors, exchanges are also building in the ability for publishers to create private exchanges. This is sort of a hybrid of premium direct-ad sales and exchange-based buying. In a private exchange, the publisher can choose to only white list certain advertisers or media buyers that they know bring high quality (and premium prices) to the auction. They can then negotiate different types of deals with these select buyers. However, once the terms are negotiated both the publisher and the advertiser get the advantage of using the more efficient exchange mechanism instead of having to run individually negotiated and manually managed campaigns.

CHAPTER 10

Retargeting Meets Social Media

The Facebook Exchange

We've described how the online-advertising landscape matured from 2007 to today in order to support a new, more sophisticated form of online ad buying in real-time bidding (RTB). In parallel, an exciting new platform emerged that was capturing a huge percentage of online traffic. Facebook set out to change the way people use the Internet to connect and share. By all accounts, it has been incredibly successful in that mission. It was also incredibly successful in attracting more users than any other social network in the history of the web. In fact, in 2012, one-third of all ad impressions served were served on Facebook. That's an incredible concentration of users on a single platform.

As a result, Facebook emerged as a powerful vehicle for advertising with innovative targeting capabilities and never-before-seen ad units. For the first time, ads became social, allowing potential customers to comment on them, share them, and communicate directly with the brand.

The first way that advertisers gained access to these ads units on Facebook was through something called *Facebook Marketplace Ads*. The Facebook Marketplace allowed advertisers to target potential customers based on information in the users' profiles (age, relationship status, education, gender, interests, etc.) or specific actions taken on Facebook (what the user has "liked," articles that users have shared, etc.). Facebook was able to do this because it created a social graph, which keeps track of every interaction any Facebook user has on Facebook, whether with other users or with brands.

FIGURE 10.1   Advertise on Facebook

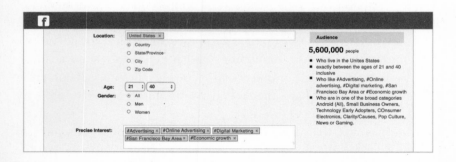

FIGURE 10.2   Sample Targeting Options on Facebook Marketplace

While this data around demographics and interests was incredibly powerful, it still kept Facebook cut off from the advancements happening around real-time bidding, personalized retargeting, and a number of new cutting-edge marketing tactics.

The Facebook Exchange (FBX) changed all that. When officially launched in June 2012, FBX made it possible to bring the sophistication of RTB to the most widely used and highly engaging platform on the web. As a result, FBX has quickly become a near requirement for any ROI-driven marketer.

For the first time ever, advertisers could use customer-intent data gathered from their websites for retargeting on Facebook. (Note: Facebook later added retargeting as a feature within the Facebook Marketplace). More importantly, marketers could now take what they know about their customers' interactions with their site, and use that to create highly engaging, one-to-one communications at scale.

FACEBOOK MARKETPLACE VERSUS FBX

It's important to note that there are some key differences between Facebook Marketplace and FBX. They are very much two separate entities, and support different functionality.

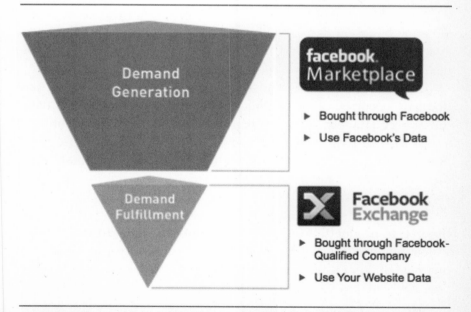

FIGURE 10.3 Understanding the Differences between Facebook Marketplace and FBX

The first major difference is how an advertiser must access these different ad products. Facebook Marketplace can be accessed directly through Facebook, which supports a self-service model, allowing advertisers to do things like create their ads, select their targeting criteria, and specify how much that they want to spend. However, you can also access Facebook Marketplace through a variety of partners. This group of companies includes something called PMDs, which stands for *Preferred Marketing Developer*. These companies are Facebook specialists, and can help advertisers employ best practices and ensure that marketers are maximizing ROI. They will often handle most of the heavy lifting associated with campaign setup and management as well.

FBX, on the other hand, requires that you work with a qualified partner, which is currently limited to about 20 companies. These companies are carefully selected based on their technical abilities, and the unique value that they bring to the Facebook platform. These partners must all have their own bidding technology, and must be able to handle the scale of ad impressions that Facebook creates.

Another major distinction is the type of targeting that each of these products supports. As we mentioned, Marketplace supports targeting based on demographic information in a user's profile, interests, and anything garnered from an interaction within the Facebook platform.

Conversely, FBX allows advertisers to use data from interactions that have occurred off of Facebook. This includes on-site intent data, third-party data sets, and any other data that an advertiser might have access to. The important thing to note here is that you cannot combine data from off of Facebook with data from on Facebook. That means that you cannot access demographic data or interest data via FBX.

Another difference is the types of ad units supported between these two products. Marketplace supports almost every ad type, which includes things like sponsored stories and page-post ads. The one type of ad unit that is not supported via Marketplace is dynamic creative.

FIGURE 10.4   Right-Hand Side Ads on Facebook

When Facebook initially debuted FBX, the only ad unit available was right-hand side (RHS) ads. At first, only static ads were supported, however Facebook quickly added support for dynamic ads in the right-hand side.

FIGURE 10.5   Dynamic Ads in the Right-Hand Side of Facebook

FACEBOOK NEWS FEED EXPLAINED

Once FBX began to pick up steam, Facebook quickly added access to its most premium placement, the News Feed, through FBX. Facebook's News Feed is the reason that billions of users log in to the platform each month—it's the first place people go and the place where they spend the most time. As a result, page post link ads (PPLAs) are highly visible and highly engaging units that bring the power of FBX retargeting to the News Feed.

Unlike standard page posts that can support various types of media—links, videos, photos, events, or even offers—FBX only currently supports Page Post Link Ads on desktop browsers.

As the name implies, Page Post Link Ads link to an external site rather than another Facebook Page—an important distinction that makes these units optimal for direct-response marketing. In addition to a prominent image, these units have multiple fields for marketing copy and calls to action. Their large size and central placement make them nearly impossible to miss when inserted into the News Feed.

These News Feed ad units are served as unpublished posts, sometimes referred to as *dark posts*, and cannot be seen on a Facebook page. This allows advertisers to maintain their brand voice while testing and optimizing post creative, and prevents oversaturating an audience.

FIGURE 10.6   FBX Ads in the News Feed

The next logical progression was to support dynamic-ad units in the News Feed, which FBX did in late 2013. This new exciting format on FBX gave advertisers the ability to combine the most effective display-ad targeting techniques with the most engaging ad unit on the most widely used platform. This led to unparalleled performance for online advertising campaigns. The results have been astounding, with performance frequently twice as good as News Feed static ad units. This allows marketers to combine the power of personalized dynamic creative with the premium placement of the News Feed.

FIGURE 10.7   Dynamic FBX Ads in the News Feed

An interesting nuance of News Feed ads is that they are not sold on an impression basis, but rather on an *insertion*. This is because ad units served in the News Feed are persistent, and may be viewed multiple times by the same user (as a user scrolls through content), so one insertion often has multiple views. This means that even with just the paid distribution, advertisers are getting more impressions than they would with an ad purchased at a similar CPM. But, News Feed ads receive more than just paid distribution and can receive viral social impressions.

Another interesting component of News Feed ads is that they are inherently cross device. Cross-device targeting, which we will cover in Chapter 11, is when you take information collected from a user on one device and target them with ads on a secondary device. Because of the fact that a News Feed ad simply enters the users' stream of events on Facebook, that ad will stay in their News Feed until enough events have occurred to push it out of view. So, I may see an ad in my News Feed on my work computer. When I go home and visit Facebook on my personal laptop, that ad may still be in my News Feed.

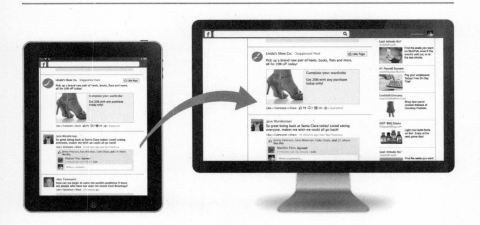

Cross-Device Ads

FIGURE 10.8   Cross-Device Ads across Facebook

Because of its prominent location, News Feed retargeting is currently limited by Facebook to only one insertion per user per day. Unlike its RHS counterpart that can serve at any frequency an advertiser specifies and can appear alongside other brand's advertisements, FBX News Feed units stand alone for maximum effect. While it's logical to limit frequency in the News Feed given its prominence, this restraint makes it necessary to complement News Feed campaigns with other inventory, like right-hand side ads as well as retargeting on the open web, to maximize overall retargeting ROI.

SOCIAL ELEMENTS

One of the key features of these ads, aside from their premium placement and response rate, is the social layer embedded in each ad. Unlike other ads, FBX News Feed ads have all the familiar Facebook social elements of page posts, allowing for unique dialogue between customer and advertiser, as well as additional viral distribution when people like, share, and comment on an ad. CTR is always going to be a good indicator of an ad's efficacy, but these social options bring a whole new measurement of success to performance-oriented campaigns. These social elements appear directly below the ad unit and are visible to the ad's target audience with each insertion. Notifications of comments on the page post will show up on a brand's Facebook page.

As a marketer, it's important to recognize that these ad units present a unique opportunity to engage your customers in a dialog. Unlike traditional web banners, which only provide broadcast communication, News Feed ads allow your customers to interact, share their point of view, or share your ad unit. You can talk to your customers and get free impressions as your customers spread the word about your brand. It's really a true convergence of direct-response advertising and social advertising.

FIGURE 10.9 **By Encouraging People to Comment and Share On Your Newsfeed Ads, Advertisers Can Extend the Ads' Reach Even Further**

COMPARING FBX TO THE REST OF THE WEB

A common question marketers ask is "How does retargeting on Facebook perform compared to the rest of the web?" While results vary depending on the vertical, customer base, and a number of other factors, we've found some interesting trends.

We analyzed campaigns from 547 advertisers serving over 1 billion ad impressions to measure how retargeting in the News Feed compared to the right-hand side FBX placements, as well as traditional display inventory from ad exchanges such as Google's DoubleClick Ad Exchange, Yahoo!'s Right Media Exchange, and AppNexus among others. We specifically looked at advertisers running FBX Right-Hand Side (RHS), FBX News Feed, and standard web retargeting. Here are some high-level stats about how each medium performs:

- News Feed retargeting had a click-through rate (CTR) 49 times higher than RHS.
- News Feed retargeting had a 21 times higher than standard web retargeting.
- News Feed CPCs were half that of RHS campaigns.
- News Feed CPCs were one-fifth of web retargeting.

The FBX study taught us a lot about how to truly drive returns across retargeting on social and open websites. Here are some high-level findings:

- News Feed and RHS complement one another and result in an overall increase in clicks at a combined lower CPC.
- News Feed alone doesn't have the reach or scale of RHS or standard web, and should therefore be used in conjunction with the other channels.
- News Feed has different applications from RHS. It's ideal for content marketing and promotions (which can capitalize on social features) while RHS is best suited for dynamic-product ads driving direct response.

One of the biggest reasons to run retargeting both on the web and FBX is that the inventory sources reach different audiences. Because

FBX News Feed is essentially the same audience as FBX RHS, we wondered whether the campaigns were driving incremental traffic. To help answer this question, we compiled data from a set of 258 advertisers as they launched retargeting campaigns in the News Feed. We found that in the first seven days after advertisers launched, News Feed ads helped raise total clicks from FBX advertising by 62 percent, helping to prove that News Feed campaigns drive incremental visits and conversions. Additionally, in these seven days the average CPC on FBX for these advertisers decreased by 30 percent.

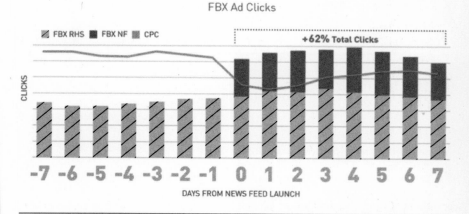

FIGURE 10.10   Using Both News Feed and Right-Hand Side Ads Drive Incremental Clicks and a Lower CPC

TWITTER ENTERS THE RETARGETING GAME

In the fourth quarter of 2013 Twitter opened their platform to allow for retargeting. Their product is still evolving so advertisers getting in now will get in on the ground floor. Like Facebook's early stance on FBX, they are using partners for this channel. As the product evolves this may change, but at the time of writing working with companies like AdRoll is necessary for launching retargeting on Twitter. You are also able to use multiple-audience segments on Twitter; for example, you can create one retargeting segment for users who have visited the appliance section of your website and another for users who have visited the computer section of your website.

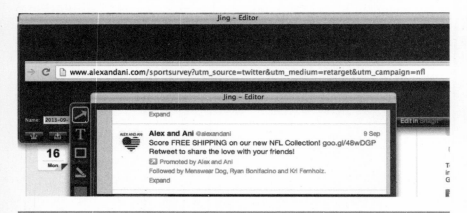

FIGURE 10.11   Twitter Retargeting Ad from Leading Retailer Alex and Ani

Twitter Case Study

Having already used Twitter ads as a great way to drive awareness and virtual event attendance, a leading B2B-technology company was looking for additional ways to use Twitter, particularly to drive incremental leads. Retargeting on Twitter looked like the perfect fit. During a one-month test campaign, they were able to reach 70,000 users. The engagement rate of retargeting on Twitter was two times that of standard Twitter ads. Click-through rates on the retargeting ads were 19 percent—72 percent more than the standard 11 percent Twitter ad click-through rate they were experiencing. They also found that leads from retargeting on Twitter were completely incremental to other channels. On average, other advertisers have seen an increase in engagement of 170 percent and a reduction in acquisition costs of 74 percent since launching retargeting on Twitter.

GETTING STARTED USING RETARGETING ACROSS SOCIAL CHANNELS

Now that you know more about how retargeting on social media works, we want to walk you through a few best practices that will help get you started.

Retarget across Inventory Sources for Better Results

As we mentioned earlier in the chapter, retargeting on social should not be used in isolation. To drive as many sales as possible, brands should retarget across social channels as well as the open web. For example, we've seen retargeting across inventory sources twice as many conversions as on Facebook alone.

Retargeting Across Social and Open Web

► Web and FBX overlap is small.

► Running across platforms results in a 34 percent lower CPA than Google alone.

► Cross platform retargeting drives 156 percent more conversions than Google alone.

► FBX plus site retargeting drives two times more conversions than FBX alone.

FIGURE 10.12   Retargeting across Social and the Open Web Is a Powerful Combination

Rotate Creatives Often to Drive Results

Creative burnout happens more quickly when retargeting on social channels, particularly RHS ads on Facebook versus retargeting across the open web, so it is important to rotate creatives regularly. The general rule of thumb is to rotate creative every two to three weeks, but this can vary by advertiser. Keep a close eye on click-through rate deterioration over time and use this as a guide for how often your brand should swap in new creative.

Use LiquidAds Whenever There Is a Product Feed

As mentioned earlier in the chapter, the use of dynamic ads in both Facebook's RHS and News Feed placements are a great way to increase click-through rates and conversion rates. While this is also true for creatives on the open web, dynamic ads are even easier to set up on Facebook, as creative resources are minimal.

Appliances Online

Appliances Online is the leading online appliance retailer in Australia. They wanted to increase their reach and drive incremental sales by retargeting across the general web and on Facebook Exchange. To do so, they launched a retargeting campaign using LiquidAds and creating customized segments for users who abandoned the shopping cart and who viewed multiple products (1+, 3+, or 6+ product viewed campaigns). By showing users the products that they viewed in the Facebook ads AppliancesOnline.com.au increased ad CTR by four times versus static retargeting ads. The cost per click on dynamic ads was also one-fifth that of static ads. LiquidAds proved to be a huge success for the company, driving ROI 14 times higher.

Engage Your Audience in the Newsfeed

As mentioned earlier in this chapter, it is important to consider the medium when using the Newsfeed as part of your retargeting strategy. Comments and shares will drive incremental impressions beyond your retargeting campaign. Consider this as you plan your strategy. This can work well as part of a loyalty or community strategy. For example, after someone buys your product, try a retargeting campaign, thanking them and encouraging them to join your loyalty program to receive updates.

CONCLUSION

Retargeting across social is a key component in broader retargeting campaigns. This allows you to reach the 17 percent of users who are only accessible on Facebook and get in front of your prospective customers where they already are. If you haven't tried this already, give it a try.

CHAPTER 11

Mobile Retargeting

Opportunities and Challenges

The next time that you find yourself in a public place, observe the people around you. Look at people on the train, at cafes, or in the airport. You'll see the tops of a lot of heads. Everyone's faces will be pointed at a mobile device of one kind or another. Reading articles, checking your e-mail, browsing the web, playing Scrabble, scrolling through Facebook; there is almost nothing that we do on our desktop computers that we cannot do on these devices today. They are our source of entertainment, information, and connection. That's why it's not surprising that by the end of 2014 it is predicted that more than half of all online behavior will occur on a mobile device. Fifty-six percent of American adults own a smartphone, and 34 percent own a tablet. The mobile device is becoming the primary device for accessing the web, and marketers need to catch up.

OPTIMIZE YOUR MOBILE EXPERIENCE

In Chapter 4, "Smart Targeting: Reach the Right People at the Right Time," we discussed how important it is to know your customers. As a marketer, you need to pay attention to how your customers are accessing your website. What percentage are browsing products on mobile devices? Which devices? How are they finding your site on these devices? What are they doing once on the site? What do your metrics look like for mobile users versus traditional web? Are your bounce rates higher? Conversion rates lower?

The reality is that people are spending more time than ever online. That means that there are more opportunities to market your brand to those people in a targetable and measurable way than ever. The problem is that while consumers are rapidly adopting the mobile device as their primary source for all things web, marketers are not adapting the experience of their site, nor are they adapting their marketing strategies, to account for this shift.

Optimizing your site for mobile traffic is no longer an optional undertaking. It is becoming as important as having a solid SEO/SEM strategy. It will become as important as having a sophisticated approach to e-mail marketing. Think about it this way; if your site is not optimized for mobile traffic, and you are spending money on search and e-mail (both of which have huge adoption on mobile devices), then you are throwing away dollars. Would you drive users to a page on your traditional site that hasn't been optimized? Would you purposefully send an e-mail linking to a broken landing page? Of course not. But if your site isn't optimized for mobile, then chances are that you're doing that every day.

One strategy to ensure that your site will work across a variety of devices is to leverage *responsive design*. Responsive design is an approach to web design that allows your site to scale gracefully to different screen sizes and resolutions. A responsive site will maintain its usability in any size browser window. It generally won't look the same on all screens, but the navigation will still be easy to access, the main call to action will be prominent, and so on. The point is, with responsive design you don't diminish the user experience on smaller screens.

FIGURE 11.1   Responsive Design Example, AdRoll.Com/About/ Careers

Another approach is called *device aware*. This means that your site has the ability to detect the device type that is accessing your site, and customize the experience accordingly. This is where understanding your customer is incredibly important. The reason that your customers access your site from a desktop might be different than the reason that they access your site on their phone. If you know the main action taken on your site on mobile devices, you can make that most prominent, therefore enhancing the user experience.

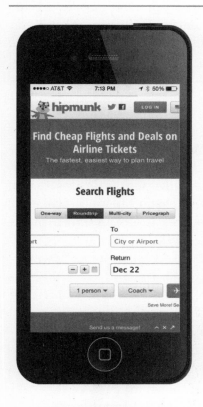

BEFORE

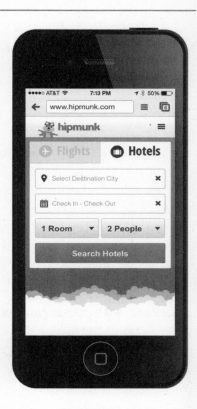

AFTER

FIGURE 11.2   What Mobile Looks Like for Hipmunk

A great example of this would be retailers that have both an online and offline presence. If I'm accessing the retailer's site on my desktop computer, chances are that I'm doing a bit of online shopping. However, if I'm accessing it on my phone, I might be looking for a retail location. If, as a marketer, after looking at my mobile-usage data, I find that a large percentage of my mobile traffic was hitting the find-store-location link, I'd want to make that very prominent on mobile devices, as that will drive more people to my retail locations, and therefore drive offline sales.

Another benefit of device-aware design is that it allows you to cut down on images, Flash movies, or anything else that might eat up bandwidth and slow your site down. One reason that the mobile web has taken off is the insatiable desire for immediate information. That means that mobile-web consumers are not willing to sit around and wait for your site to load. Keep it light and simple, with the most frequently used features most prominent and buttons large enough to account for our clumsy thumbs.

MOBILE PAYMENTS

People are beginning to make purchases on their mobile devices. In fact, in the 2013 *Mobile Path to Purchase* study conducted by Nielsen, xAd, and Telmetrics, 46 percent of smartphone users had used their smartphone exclusively during the purchase process.

However, small screens and tiny keyboards present another problem; typing in your payment information is incredibly tedious. For this reason, another challenge that marketers face while addressing their mobile customers is optimizing the mobile-payment process.

To date, there is no great solution to this problem. A data point that backs this up is the fact that 74 percent of smartphone users who researched a product on their phone completed that purchase offline in a retail store location.

That said, a lot of companies are working on this exact problem. Companies like PayPal, Amazon, Google, and Square are all addressing this problem in one way or another. There are also solutions out there that let your customers upload their payment information by taking a photo of their credit card. If you're looking to drive purchases on your mobile site, make sure that you have streamlined your mobile checkout process as much as possible.

MOBILE AS THE POINT OF INTENT

A very interesting trend emerging in mobile is that consumers are using their mobile devices to research products and services. That means that mobile is becoming a place where your customers are exhibiting intent signals. The previously referenced study found that 50 percent of smartphone users start their research process on their phones. Mobile now represents one-third of all online-shopping behavior. A behavior that has been written about at length is something called *showrooming*. Showrooming is when a customer is in a store looking at a particular product, while simultaneously comparison-shopping online. There has been a bit of a debate about how prevalent this is, with Google releasing a study that found this to be very common, while the *Mobile Path to Purchase* study stated that it was more common for shoppers to comparison shop on their mobile devices either before entering the store, or after leaving.

Regardless of when it is happening, it's important to understand if this applies to your customer base even if you don't have brick-and-mortar retail locations. For example, if your competitors have retail locations, chances are that their customers are showrooming. Understanding this gives you the opportunity to market to them when they do so.

CAPTURING INTENT ON MOBILE DEVICES

One of the largest challenges with mobile retargeting is the fact that cookies don't function as well in a mobile environment. Cookies, previously described in Chapter 2 as the current backbone for tracking intent in web browsers, do work in mobile browsers, but there is a caveat. Safari, which represents about 54 percent of mobile browser adoption globally, blocks third-party cookies by default. This means that most of the retargeting companies out there aren't able to use cookies to capture intent in Safari. In other words, 54 percent of the time that a mobile web user exhibits intent, it is ignored by most online advertising companies.

Additionally, cookies don't function in mobile-app environments, and therefore can't be relied on to capture intent in mobile applications. As a result, alternative types of IDs have been created to account for in-app behavior. However, those IDs vary based on device maker and operating system, so there is no operating-system-agnostic ID that mobile-ad exchanges can use to identify users.

Apple has created an ID specifically for advertisers, referred to as IDFA (ID for Advertisers). IDFA provides a way for advertising companies to track intent within mobile apps, without being able to link that ID to any personally identifiable information. This ID is also configurable, so if a web consumer doesn't wish to be tracked, he or she can indicate as much. Many of the mobile-ad networks and exchanges have adopted this ID for the purpose of online-behavioral advertising.

Once you understand how your customers are interacting with your company on their mobile devices you can begin to craft a strategy to capitalize on the intent signals that they're exhibiting. We've described the challenges at length, but not to discourage you from experimenting in mobile. By understanding the limitations, you can tailor your strategy to account for these challenges. Mobile is also packed with exciting opportunities. So how can you take advantage of this increasing web adoption to reach these customers on their mobile devices?

MOBILE-WEB TO MOBILE-WEB RETARGETING

According to one study by Nielsen, the majority of online-mobile activity in the United States is still on the mobile web. Take a look at the breakdown of mobile activity by country from the most recent Nielsen Mobile Consumer Activity Report.

Other reports contradict this, placing app usage as the dominant medium. While it varies by country, it is important to note that mobile-web usage is still a major component of smartphone and tablet usage. As a marketer, you should factor this into your strategy.

The simplest and most common form of mobile retargeting is mobile web to mobile web. This occurs when one of your customers visits your website in a mobile browser. Assuming that you have retargeting placed on your mobile website, you are able to capture that customer's browsing behavior for all mobile browsers besides Safari. Then, when that customer is visiting their favorite mobile site or blog, you are able to retarget them on that site. It functions much like traditional web retargeting but with the challenges outlined previously.

Activities performed by smartphone users at least once a month, according to Nielsen							
	SMS	Web browsing	Email	Social networking	Apps	Streaming music	Instant messaging	Video/mobile TV
Australia	94%	60%	55%	58%	59%	21%	33%	19%
Brazil	85%	69%	66%	75%	74%	39%	57%	43%
China	84%	75%	58%	62%	71%	59%	67%	39%
India	45%	15%	17%	26%	13%	11%	15%	8%
Italy	89%	37%	51%	47%	49%	26%	35%	17%
Russia	95%	68%	55%	59%	64%	41%	34%	36%
South Korea	93%	80%	52%	55%	81%	40%	70%	44%
Turkey	78%	37%	33%	69%	38%	22%	50%	9%
UK	92%	66%	68%	63%	56%	20%	37%	19%
United States	86%	82%	75%	63%	62%	38%	28%	28%

FIGURE 11.3 Nielsen Study on Mobile Activity in the United States

Source: Adapted from www.nielsen.com/us/en/reports/2013/mobile-consumer-report-february-2013.html.

FIGURE 11.4   Mobile-Web to Mobile-Web Retargeting

The mobile web is becoming more sophisticated, with many website publishers focusing on optimizing the mobile experience. Publishers are frequently using the device-aware approach to offer mobile-specific ad units. As a result, it's best practice to include these mobile-specific ad formats in your retargeting campaigns. The most common of these is the 320×50. Every year, the Internet Advertising Bureau (IAB) releases its list of Mobile Rising Stars Ad Units that details the new mobile-ad formats that are gaining traction and driving performance.

APP-TO-APP RETARGETING

While mobile web represents a large percentage of mobile usage, apps continue to thrive. When developing your mobile strategy, you'll have to decide if developing a mobile app is right for your business. There are advantages, such as being able to save payment information to ease the checkout process, but the decision whether to build an app or not will largely depend on the product or service that you offer, your customers' needs, and a number of other factors.

App-to-app retargeting occurs when a brand has a native mobile application for their customers. This is very common within the travel, banking, and flash-sale verticals, among others. When a mobile-device user visits one of these applications, that app is able to capture any intent signals exhibited in that app. Then, as that customer interacts with other apps, perhaps to play a mobile game or browse Facebook, the brand is able to target that user with mobile ads.

FIGURE 11.5   In-App Retargeting

An interesting trend in mobile app retargeting is something called *deep linking*. Deep linking is a borrowed tactic from standard-web retargeting in which you direct a user back to the exact page that they abandoned. While this may seem very basic, it is something that was previously very difficult to do in the app ecosystem. One problem is that by linking directly to your app, you are assuming that the app is installed on that device. There is always the chance that the user removed the app, in which case the experience of clicking through would be broken. For this reason, marketers have shied away from deep linking and instead opted towards directing people to their mobile website. We are not going to cover deep linking in detail here, but just know that it is possible, has advantages, and requires someone technical to handle its implementation.

RETARGETING BETWEEN BROWSERS AND APPS

One of the main problems with mobile retargeting is that most brands don't have apps, yet a lot of the available advertising impressions are in mobile apps. In an ideal world, as a marketer you'd be able to track behavior that happens on your mobile website and target users as they interact with different apps on their phone or tablet. This is retargeting between browsers and apps. However, it has a number of technical challenges associated with it.

The biggest technical challenge is a result of the fact that mobile devices make it very difficult to associate your mobile web-browsing history with your app activity. We've already discussed how the backbone of web tracking is the cookie, which doesn't function in mobile apps. Conversely, as a marketer, you cannot access the device-specific IDs, like Apple's IDFA, from the mobile browser. As a result, it's incredibly difficult to determine if the person who visited your mobile site 30 minutes ago is the same person playing *Words with Friends* right now.

There are two ways that ad-tech companies are attempting to solve this problem. The first is through a probabilistic model. When your device fires up an app or the browser, a number of signals are sent to the application that is initiating. This could be things like the Wi-Fi network this device is connected to, IP address, or user agent. There are a number of signals that are taken into account, and these models attempt to say with a certain level of accuracy that this mobile-web user and this mobile-app user are indeed the same person. However, to date, there are questions as to how accurate these models are, and if they will be able to eventually make that association with certainty.

The other, more accurate way of doing this is through something called *common login*. There are a number of services that many people log into via the web, as well as through a specific app. E-mail, social networks, banks, and dating sites are all great examples. What common login does is leverage the username to associate a web cookie with a mobile device ID.

For example, let's say that I log in to my favorite social network via the mobile web on my tablet. The social network sets a cookie in my browser as a result of this. Once I'm logged in, they prompt me to install the app for that social network, which I do. Then I log in via the app, which is able to recognize my IDFA. Now, that social network is able to associate a web cookie that it set in my browser with the IDFA ID that it read when I logged in via the app. That allows that network to retarget my web behavior as I browse other apps.

Common login is a very accurate, effective way to bridge between apps and browsers. However, there are only a few companies that are positioned to do so at scale. Large social networks and e-mail providers are best positioned to support this, as they have a large number of users accessing their products from multiple devices.

CROSS-DEVICE RETARGETING

Building on this idea of bridging between mobile browsers and mobile apps is something called *cross-device retargeting*. Cross-device retargeting takes it one step further by allowing advertisers to capture an intent signal on one device, like your laptop, and then target that user when they are browsing the web on a second device, such as their tablet.

Cross-device retargeting is often referred to as the Holy Grail. This is because at this point, it is incredibly hard to do accurately, but would be very powerful. Here's why: Let's say that I'm at work on my laptop and I receive an e-mail for a sale on my favorite flash site. I may click through, browse a product, and even put it in my shopping cart. But then a meeting invite goes off, and I have to run off to a conference room. That night when I get home and am browsing the web on my tablet, I might have more time to complete that purchase. Cross-device retargeting allows the marketer to reach me then, when I am more likely to buy.

The probabilistic model described previously becomes even more complicated when applied to cross-device retargeting, but the principles are the same. The signals might change, but companies attempting this approach are creating models that attempt to associate multiple devices with a single user based on a number of commonalities between those devices.

Again, common login is the most accurate way to make this association, as there are a number of services that users likely log in to on multiple devices. We expect this to be a major focus of 2014, and for marketers to have access to this powerful type of retargeting more broadly.

RETARGETING TACTICS IN MOBILE

Now that we've covered the major challenges, as well as defined the various types of mobile retargeting, lets take a quick look at a few different applications of mobile retargeting.

- Driving app installs: If your company has a mobile app, you may want to capture customers browsing your mobile website and drive them to install your mobile app. You can do this by targeting users with ads that direct them to the app store.
- Cross-promoting apps: If you have multiple apps, you could easily run an app-to-app retargeting campaign designed to promote additional apps in your portfolio.
- Drive app engagement: Use retargeting to bring people back to your app to engage or take a specific action.
- Drive purchases or leads: Whether you've decided to focus on optimizing your site for mobile, or on building a mobile app, the reality is that people are starting to warm up to the idea of making purchases on their mobile devices. Once you've streamlined your checkout process for your mobile audience, begin using retargeting to drive purchases or leads.
- Branding: While retargeting is predominantly known as a performance channel, mobile presents some interesting opportunities to leverage retargeting for the purpose of branding. Don't be afraid to get creative with your mobile campaign. These devices have different capabilities than their desktop counterparts, like cameras. How can you change your strategy to take advantage of that?

We could write an entire book on the challenges and opportunities within mobile, but we just wanted to provide some insights into how important it is to start thinking about how mobile fits into your brand's overall strategy. As with your desktop strategy, it all starts with understanding your users. If your customers are mobile heavy, or if you're starting to see an increase in traffic to your site from mobile devices, then it's time to get serious about mobile.

The other important thing to note is that the mobile landscape is changing incredibly fast. It's our opinion that the challenges that we've highlighted will be solved within the next couple of years, if not faster. As a marketer, you always want to be in front of changes in technology, so even if mobile isn't a significant source of traffic today, it probably makes sense to start developing a strategy.

CHAPTER 12

Aligning Your E-mail and Retargeting Strategies

Throughout this this book, we've talked a lot about the different strategies for using retargeting to drive a desired action. E-mail has historically been an incredibly effective channel for this as well. The best marketers are finding creative ways for these two channels to complement each other. In many ways, your e-mail strategy should be very similar to your retargeting strategy. The best e-mail campaigns are targeted based on an action that a customer has taken in the past. Maybe that customer signed up for a free trial but never converted to paid. In this case you would probably send an activation e-mail to that user. Maybe a person purchased something in the past but hasn't engaged with your brand in a while, so you send an e-mail with a special offer to bring them back to your site. Sound familiar? It should, because that describes some common retargeting strategies that we've covered in this book.

For many marketers, the e-mail-send lists that they are creating line up pretty well with the retargeting segments that they are creating. But what are some of the leading ways to tie these two channels together?

CRM RETARGETING

We touched upon CRM retargeting briefly in Chapter 4. As a reminder, CRM (Customer Relationship Management) retargeting is a relatively new channel that allows marketers to associate cookies with customers in their e-mail database so that they can target them with display ads as they browse sites on the web. This association is made by a handful of companies who have created partnerships with sites that require users to log in, like a social network or dating site. Let's take a dating site as an example.

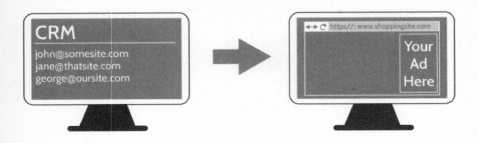

FIGURE 12.1   How CRM Retargeting Works

When I log into a dating site, I input my e-mail address on the login page. That allows the dating site to know who I am. At the same time, that allows the company that has partnered with the dating site to associate a cookie with my e-mail address, which they anonymize by hashing it and storing it in a database.

Now that there is a web cookie associated with my e-mail address, it's not difficult to find me as I travel around the web. So, let's say that I've signed up for a new flash-sale site. However, I haven't bought anything, and in fact it's been months since I've visited the site. The marketing manager from the flash-sale site wants to engage with me, so she sends me an e-mail. But she also decides to launch a CRM-retargeting campaign, and uploads a list of e-mail address (including mine) to her retargeting provider. Her retargeting provider has associated a cookie with my e-mail address, which means that when I visit Facebook or one of my favorite news sites, I see ads for the flash-sale site offering me free shipping on my first order.

Now that we understand what CRM retargeting is, let's look at some practical applications.

RE-ENGAGE PAST PURCHASERS

One of the best applications of CRM retargeting is reengaging people who've purchased from your site in the past. This assumes that you capture e-mail upon checkout.

Let's say that you are the marketing manager for a women's apparel site. Last Memorial Day you ran a very successful sale. In your database you have a list of people who purchased something from that sale and their e-mails. Now, Labor Day is coming, and you are planning a similar sale. That list of people who purchased something during the Memorial Day sale is incredibly valuable, and as a savvy marketer you send an e-mail announcing that sale to that list.

CRM retargeting allows you to launch a display campaign to that same audience. So while that e-mail that you send might end up in a spam folder or an e-mail account that is rarely checked, you can engage those past purchasers as they are catching up on an article on *The Huffington Post* or scrolling through their feed on Facebook. It is a powerful complement to your e-mail campaign and allows you to launch a cross-channel campaign with consistent messaging to an audience that has shown interest in your company.

> CRM retargeting is a great tactic to re-engage past purchasers and go higher up the marketing funnel. A leading men's-clothing company used CRM retargeting to expose their products to past purchasers who had not bought anything in more than six months. Although the average click-through rate and average cost per acquisition were higher than their standard site-retargeting campaigns, they saw this as a great way to reach a broader audience. At roughly a .2 percent CTR and a $5 CPA, their average CTR and CPA were lower than their other forms of online advertising.

REACTIVATE DORMANT USERS

E-mail has always been the go-to channel for reactivation. Any service that relies on active users to drive ad revenue leverages e-mail to bring people back to their site. CRM retargeting is a strong complement to this type of campaign as well. Let's use a free social network that relies on advertising revenue as an example.

Myfriendsfacespace.com is a free social network. They have a problem in which users sign up, poke around for a month, but then lose interest and stop engaging with the product. The marketing team at Myfriendsfacespace.com is spending a ton of money on new-user acquisition, but the lifetime value of those users is very low as a result of the fact that they aren't sticking around.

The marketing team decides to launch an e-mail campaign to re-activate users who have not logged in for months. Simultaneously, they launch a CRM-retargeting campaign with the same message targeting the same users. This allows them to stay top of mind when their users are spending time browsing sites on the web, rather than just when they open their inbox first thing in the morning.

Die-hard music fans know everything about when their favorite artists are touring, but what about everyone else? A large music act was looking for ways to let past concert goers know that their tour was rolling into various cities across the United States. They've always used e-mail marketing as a way to do this, but they were looking for more exposure for their tour. They looked to CRM retargeting as a way to increase awareness of their national tour and ultimately drive concert sales. With CRM retargeting, in a short period of time, they drove over 500,000 impressions to people who had previously attended past concerts and had the highest propensity to buy. They also increased ticket sales in key cities.

LEAD NURTURING

Lead nurturing is a tactic in the B2B space that is designed to drive would-be customers through the sign-up or purchase process. It often involves things like lead-capture forms, gated content, and other strategies to convince potential customers to offer up their e-mail addresses. Once they've obtained an e-mail address, those marketers can engage with those would-be customers with a series of e-mails designed to drive the next desired action.

Historically the exclusive channel for lead nurturing has been e-mail. However, CRM retargeting has brought display advertising into the mix. The same triggers that marketers use to decide which e-mails to send can be used to decide which retargeting ads to display. Again, this allows marketers to take an effective strategy and apply it to multiple channels.

CRM retargeting is a particularly powerful new marketing tactic because it allows marketers to re-engage with customers who have not been to their site in a while. E-mails, unlike cookies, are relatively persistent. That means that as long as you have a valid e-mail address for a customer, you can continue the dialog with them long after they've been to your site.

HOLIDAY PROMOTIONS

According to today.com, 6 out of 10 online retailers start holiday promotions before Halloween.[1] With competition increasing more and more every year, advertisers are looking for ways to market to the people with the highest likelihood of purchasing. In many cases, your past customers are the most likely to buy your product or service and getting in front of this audience is key to driving incremental holiday sales. With CRM retargeting, you can target past purchasers before they come back to your site and get in front of them before your competitors do.

FIGURE 12.2   Get in Front of the Holiday Shopping Season with CRM Retargeting

[1]www.today.com/money/happy-halloween-now-lets-talk-holiday-shopping-1C6779077.

Let's say it is October and you are an online retailer with an e-mail database of 500,000 records and each record represents a past purchaser. E-mail marketing is a key part to your holiday marketing strategy, but what if there was more that you could do to increase holiday sales? As you segment your e-mail database, create similar CRM retargeting segments. Use the same messaging and look and feel across both e-mail and retargeting ads to help reinforce the message and strengthen performance across channels.

E-MAIL RETARGETING

E-mail retargeting occurs when a marketer places a retargeting tag in an e-mail template that can detect that a customer has opened that e-mail. This is the same way that ESPs are able to report on what percentage of your e-mail send list opened the e-mails. When the customer opens the e-mail, he or she is cookied, and added to a retargeting segment. That segment of users can then be shown display ads as they travel the web.

There are some major limitations associated with e-mail retargeting. First of all, a very small percentage of marketing e-mails that are sent actually get opened (all the more reason to complement that e-mail send with CRM retargeting!). But what further complicates matters is the fact that most e-mail products block images by default. Retargeting tags in e-mails are tiny images, and therefore, unless the user either clicks display images or sets his/her default to allow images to load, that retargeting pixel will not load. If that's the case, that user will not be cookied, and will not be added to a retargeting segment.

If you think about the fact that a small percentage of customers who you e-mail will actually open that e-mail, and an even smaller percentage will do so with cookies enabled, you are probably looking at a pretty small subset of targetable customers. As a result, this tactic is best suited for larger companies with very large e-mail send lists.

MARKETING AUTOMATION

Marketing automation refers to automated e-mails that are sent based on a trigger or action taken by a potential customer. Historically it has applied to the enterprise-B2B world, but there are a few companies that are looking to make this accessible to smaller brands and appeal to other vertical markets.

If your company is already leveraging marketing automation to send e-mails, it is a great opportunity to align your retargeting strategy with your e-mail strategy. To do so, create segments for each of the events that triggers an e-mail. Then create display ads that contain the same imagery, messaging, and call to action contained in that e-mail. Direct users to the same landing page, and launch your retargeting campaign. If the next desired action triggers another e-mail, be sure to create a segment for that action as well, and exclude it from this campaign so that users aren't seeing ads driving them to take an action that they've already taken. Then, launch a second campaign targeting that segment associated with the second event, and so on.

E-mail and retargeting are both great channels for driving sales. As a marketer, aligning your strategy between these two channels allows you to ensure that your customers are seeing a consistent message, and that you are not overweighted on a single channel. E-mail faces some new challenges as inboxes are becoming more crowded and products like Gmail have begun to separate promotional e-mails into their own section of the inbox. By aligning your retargeting strategy with your e-mail strategy, you can ensure that your message is making its way to your customers.

CHAPTER 13

Privacy Matters

Providing Transparency and Control

The online ecosystem is driven by advertising dollars. Today you can get the world's news, watch viral videos, or video chat with your loved ones from the other side of the planet without having to take out your credit card. E-mail is free. Facebook is free. Wikipedia is free. Online advertising is the currency that has allowed these services to thrive by delivering them at no cost to the consumer. It's pretty incredible when you think about just how much you can learn, do, and experience via the Internet without spending a dollar.

For much of this book, we've discussed how by understanding and capturing intent signals, marketers are able to run highly effective and ROI positive campaigns. This premise is based entirely on the ability to track the online behavior of web users. Along with this incredibly powerful capability comes a tremendous amount of responsibility. Any company that leverages data derived from the browsing habits of web users is obligated to also allow consumers who are not comfortable with such tracking to raise their hand and say "I do not wish to be tracked." Any company that collects and uses online-behavioral data must also explicitly allow web users to opt out of participating in that data collection and usage.

As a reminder, online-behavioral advertising (OBA) is defined as:

> the practice of collecting data from a particular computer or device regarding web viewing behaviors over time and across nonaffiliate websites for the purpose of using such data to predict user preferences or interests to deliver advertising to

that computer or device based on the preferences or interests inferred from such Web viewing behaviors.

—http://www.aboutads.info/

The policies and regulations that we are going to discuss in this chapter apply to any company that participates in such advertising, including retargeting, third-party data targeting, or any number of other data-driven display products.

WHY IS PRIVACY IMPORTANT?

When we discuss online privacy, we are really discussing the ability for all web users to know what data is being collected about them, and then to take control of that data collection. This can be boiled down to something referred to as *transparency and control*. We'll discuss these two tenets of consumer privacy in detail, but first let's take a look at why adhering to them is important.

Providing transparency and control is essential to build trust between brands and consumers. Often, simply by clearly stating what information is being collected, you are able to dispel any fears regarding tracking. In most cases, consumers are more concerned about the idea of being tracked, then they are about the actual data being collected. Once they understand that cookie-based tracking is anonymous and temporary, they are often fine with the elements of their browsing history that are being captured. This is evident based on the extremely small percentage of people who actually opt out of OBA targeting.

Providing clear control over the collection and usage of this data is a signal to consumers that you only wish to include them in your advertising campaigns if they wish to participate. If not, you respect their decision and will remove them from your campaigns. It's analogous to someone unsubscribing from one of your e-mail sends or adding themselves to your do-not-call list. In fact, it's beneficial if people who do not wish to participate opt out. That might sound counterintuitive. However, if this is someone who doesn't wish to participate, chances are that they would not have reacted favorably to your online-advertising campaign. By removing them from the campaign, you can reallocate your advertising dollars to potential customers who will be more receptive to your message.

The most important reason that privacy matters is simply because providing transparency and control is the right thing to do. The reality is that crafty technologists can find ways around the regulations and policies. However, at the end of the day, business ethics come into play. We, as the industry that has invented these powerful tools for marketers, need to be the ones who take responsibility for them. So before you test out a new technology or product, make sure that it comes with the ability for a consumer to signal that they do not wish to participate.

WHO REGULATES THE INDUSTRY?

There are a number of organizations that are involved with making sure that companies that leverage OBA data are doing so in a responsible manner. Among them are the Digital Advertising Agency (DAA), the Internet Advertising Bureau (IAB), the National Advertising Initiative (NAI), the World Wide Web Consortium (the W3C) and the Better Business Bureau (BBB).

While this alphabet soup can be confusing to navigate, the principles set forth by the DAA have become the guiding light for the Self-Regulatory Program. The Self-Regulatory Program, which applies only to the United States, came about in response to the FTC placing the impetus of respecting consumer privacy in the hands of those in the industry, rather than passing legislation to regulate how online data is collected and acted upon.

In July 2009, the DAA published the OBA Practice Principles, a guideline by which all companies who participate in online behavioral advertising are expected to adhere. Those principles are:

Education: The Education Principle calls for the industry to put forth materials that clearly explain to consumers how online data is collected, what is collected, and how it could be used.

Transparency: The Transparency Principle requires that companies' OBA data clearly disclose and inform consumers about data collection and how that data is used for online-behavioral advertising. In order to comply with this principle, websites must disclose that data is being collected at the point of collection (where the user is cookied), as well as at the point of action (when the user is shown an advertisement leveraging OBA data).

Control: The Consumer Control Principle requires a mechanism to allow consumers to specify whether data can be collected or used for the purpose of OBA campaigns. In essence, consumers need a tool to exercise their choice regarding whether they want their data to be collected or acted upon.

Security: The Data Security Principle requires reasonable security for data collected and used for online behavioral advertising purposes.

Material Changes: The Material Changes Principle directs entities to obtain consent before applying any change to their online behavioral advertising data collection and use policy that is less restrictive to data collected prior to such material change.

Sensitive Data: The Sensitive Data Principle recognizes that certain data collected and used for online-behavioral advertising purposes merits different treatment. Specifically, there is heightened protection for children's data by applying the protective measures established in the Children's Online Privacy Protection Act. Similarly, this principle requires consent for the collection of financial account numbers, social security numbers, pharmaceutical prescriptions, or medical records about a specific individual for online-behavioral advertising purposes.

Accountability: The Accountability Principle refers to the fact that the online-advertising industry will put measures in place to ensure that companies participating in Online-Behavioral Advertising are adhering to the principles just described.

HOW TO REMAIN COMPLIANT

While all of this seems very daunting, it's actually very simple to remain compliant. Just follow these steps:

1. Provide clear language that describes what type of data is being collected on your website. Your privacy policy is the perfect place for information like this. It's also best practice to provide the ability to opt out of this data collection by displaying the *About Ads* icon (pictured below) on your site and linking to one of the organizations that offers the opt-out mechanism, such as IAB, NAI, or Evidon.

FIGURE 13.1   About Ads Icon

Source: Created by the Digital Advertising Alliance (DAA). http://www.aboutads.info/.

2. Only work with advertising companies that are members of the NAI, DAA, or IAB, and who are 100 percent compliant with the self-regulatory program. The good news is, if they are members of at least one of those organizations (often indicated by the presence of those logos on their websites) they've already been vetted as compliant. You can check the websites of the above organizations to see who the members are.

FIGURE 13.2   Clicking on This Ad Choice Icon in a Banner Ad Provides More Information about the Data That Is Collected

3. Ensure that all of your ads that are targeting online data contain the *About Ads* icon. Again, if you are working with partners who are compliant with the self-regulatory program, then they will take care of serving this icon in each ad impression. They will also ensure that it links to information about the data being collected, as well as the ability to opt out of data collection and usage.

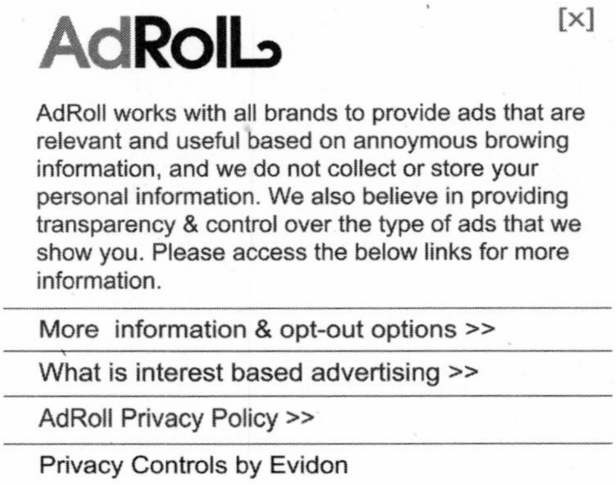

AdRoll [x]

AdRoll works with all brands to provide ads that are relevant and useful based on annoymous browing information, and we do not collect or store your personal information. We also believe in providing transparency & control over the type of ads that we show you. Please access the below links for more information.

More information & opt-out options >>

What is interest based advertising >>

AdRoll Privacy Policy >>

Privacy Controls by Evidon

FIGURE 13.3   Sample Information That Is Shown About the Ad After the Icon Is Clicked

If you follow those three rules, you'll ensure that your brand is compliant with the self-regulatory program.

DO NOT TRACK EXPLAINED

Do not track (DNT) is a browser setting that signals to online advertising companies that this user does not want to be tracked or targeted. It is an HTTP-header field that requests that web applications disable tracking of the individual user. Web users can go into their browser preferences and set this to on or off. It was developed as a proposed universal tool for opting web users out of OBA. However, it has been the source of much debate. The reason for this debate is because there has never been agreement on exactly what DNT meant. Some interpret it as Do not target, meaning that it is still okay to track data about that particular user's session. Others interpret it as data cannot be tracked for the purpose of OBA, but can be tracked for the purpose of site analytics, while some believe that all online tracking should cease if that browser header is detected.

While DNT could be the right solution to the consumer-privacy issue, until there is agreement across all parties on how that signal should be interpreted and respected, it will continue to be a source of controversy.

GLOBAL PRIVACY

Each country or region is going to have different perspectives, policies, and laws regarding consumer privacy. While there are too many nuances between each country to cover in this book, we can discuss the two camps that most countries fall into.

The first is *implied consent*. Implied consent means that web users by default, unless otherwise specified via an opt out or browser setting, accept that their data is being collected and leveraged for online behavioral advertising. Countries that accept this model include the United States and Canada.

The second is *explicit consent*. Explicit consent refers to having to ask a consumer permission for collecting any OBA data each time that they visit your site. This is much less common, but has some traction in Europe. This is currently mandated in France, Portugal, the Netherlands, Latvia, Lithuania, and Cyprus.

Europe is undergoing some changes to its approach to privacy. The European Union handed down legislation referred to as The EU ePrivacy Directive. This is an actual law (as opposed to the self-regulatory program in the United States), and requires that each country pass legislation requiring websites to provide notice when collecting or using a European consumers' data, provide the ability to control how that data is used, and request consent. To date, this has not been successfully implemented in most countries in the EU.

Europe does have a self-regulatory program as well, which is very similar to the U.S. program. The organization responsible for monitoring compliance in the EU is the European Interactive Digital Advertising Alliance.

While the topic of consumer privacy is always in the news, and a source for debate, it is not something to be overly concerned about. Just make sure that the advertising partners that you work with are members of the leading organizations. As long as you offer transparency and control, you are not at risk for any violations. If you are contacted by any of the organizations that we've described in this chapter, just work with them on becoming compliant. They are reasonable and want to help your company better understand consumer privacy. If you're nervous about the topic, enlist a company like Evidon for help getting and maintaining compliance. Evidon is a technology and service provider that helps companies participating in online advertising stay compliant.

CHAPTER 14

Conclusion

A Look to the Future

There is a short list of must-have marketing channels: SEO/SEM, house e-mail lists, and retargeting. There are few, if any other channels that have stood the test of time to show positive ROI on an ongoing basis across any advertiser size and vertical.

However, despite its place on this elite list, retargeting tactics will need to continue to evolve as consumer behaviors change and new technologies emerge. This is true of any marketing channel. The most notable shift taking place is the increased consumption of content on mobile devices. As discussed in Chapter 11, mobile presents a set of imminent challenges. It's widely known that the percent of mobile traffic generated from mobile devices is rapidly growing.

There are challenges to simply executing a retargeting campaign on mobile devices because of the different standards between devices, operating systems, and walled garden between mobile web and apps. However, this data points to a broader trend of consumers using multiple devices.

Gone are the days of being able to simply reach people on their one home computer and being able to generate a picture of the consumer journey on that one device. For example, today a person who's buying a TV might use their mobile phone to compare prices while in a brick-and-mortar store, then read reviews on their tablet when they get home, and finally purchase online from their work computer.

Clearly new technologies and techniques will have to emerge for marketers to operate with this fragmented view of a consumer. While a perfectly holistic view of the customer journey might never be totally possible, options are rapidly developing to stitch together elements of the user experience.

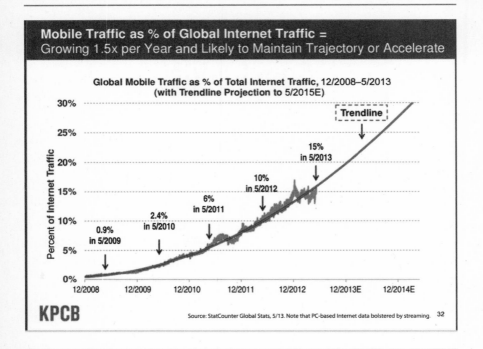

FIGURE 14.1   Mobile Traffic Trends in 2013

Source: www.slideshare.net/kleinerperkins/kpcb-internet-trends-2013.

In particular, web giants like Google, Facebook, Amazon, and Twitter who have data on users across devices are slowly making that data available to marketers for both better targeting and more accurate measurement.

NEW ENVIRONMENTS AND NEW FORMATS

The drift of users from a single desktop web experience to a fragmented experience across the web and connected apps naturally means that ad formats will change and adapt to these new experiences. A simple example of this can be seen with Facebook's inclusion of prominent News Feed placements into FBX. This was in many ways a landmark move as it brought together two of the most exciting trends in digital advertising: real-time bidding and native-ad units. Given that Facebook's mobile app only has News Feed ad placements, you can see where this trend is taking us.

Twitter is another example of a mobile-first company where the primary ad format is a native, in-feed ad unit. Similar to Facebook, Twitter also has a few consumers accessing their service from both desktops and mobile devices. This makes the recently available Twitter retargeting options inherently cross-device. Businesses can identify users who visit their desktop website, then retarget them on their mobile devices in the Twitter app.

Even television, a stalwart of traditional media is becoming fragmented. In March 2013, Nielsen reported that the number of zero-TV homes (that is, no traditional-cable or satellite-service connected device) increased from 3 million people in the United States in 2007 to 5 million people in 2013. That's still a fairly small number of the overall U.S. market, but it's growing rapidly, and the demographics point to a further shift in the future. In fact, there's a growing segment that has actually never had a subscription to cable, satellite, or other similar service.

US "No-TV" Homes

FIGURE 14.2 Growing Segment of People Who Do Not Own Televisions

Do zero-TV homes mean people aren't watching video? Of course not, they're just consuming it in different ways: Hulu, Netflix, YouTube, and countless other streaming options that only require broadband, but not cable or other traditional TV-delivery options.

While this trend might be bad news for the cable companies, it's good news for the digital marketer. TV will no longer be the private domain of mega brands with big-budget, prime-time placements nego- tiated in Madison Avenue restaurants with a martini and a handshake. The increases in digital-streaming video open this medium to the types of targeting advertisers have become accustomed to with the web.

For example, now a brand like GoPro that has fantastic user- generated video content can retarget people who looked at the latest camera on their website with the appropriate skiing videos in the win- ter or surfing videos in the summer on Youtube or other video sites. As people start to adopt devices that bring streaming to their TV, like Roku, AppleTV, and Google's ChromeCast, advertisers will be able to target and retarget people on their wall-mounted plasma screens in the same way they had historically reached them on their desktop computers.

WHAT'S NEXT FOR THE RETARGETING INDUSTRY?

So what's next for the retargeting industry? Clearly there will be further advancement in bidding algorithms, better-looking dynamic creative that delivers more accurate product recommendation, and a further trend to placement in more integrated, native environments like social feeds and mobile apps.

These improvements to existing technologies will improve adver- tiser ROI, generate more revenue for publishers, and provide a better user experience by continuing to subsidize free content with more rele- vant ads. Retargeting platforms will also adapt to unify advertising across increasingly fragmented options. Marketing professionals are busy peo- ple, and they demand tools that allow them to do things across platforms instead of having to log into multiple interfaces.

The retargeting platform of the future will have its foundation in Big Data and the ability to execute intelligent bidding based on how valu- able a particular user is to a specific brand, and be able to do that across a range of media. This will include the sources that are available today:

traditional desktop display and Facebook, but will also include emerging channels like mobile devices, new native ad units from the likes of Twitter, and within increasingly connected TVs.

In the future, marketers who master today's retargeting techniques will become even more powerful as they become able to extend these tactics to reach potential customers throughout the entire digital journey.

Glossary

above the fold: The part of a web page that is viewed without having to scroll down.

ad network: Responsible for selling the majority of ad inventory, ad networks are companies that aggregate various publisher websites, open ad inventory, and match that inventory with advertiser demand.

ad exchange: A source for display inventory where ad impressions (across a single or multiple publishers) are auctioned to a range of bidders, usually in real time as the impressions are rendered.

ad burnout: This occurs when a person has seen an ad too many times and is desensitized to its message.

banner blindness: The behavior of web users who become accustomed to the location of ad units on a website and tune out that location as they browse pages on that site.

below the fold: The part of the webpage that can only be viewed if a visitor scrolls down. Typically, ads that appear below the fold have a lower CPM than ads that appear above the fold. In the case of news sites, ads below the fold can have higher click-through rates as visitors are more engaged with site content.

cookie: A cookie is a small piece of data sent from a website and stored in a user's web browser while the user is browsing the web. The data can be read by the web domain that set the cookie until the cookie file expires or is deleted by the user.

CPC: Cost per click.

CPM: Cost per thousand impressions. Literal translation is cost per mille, which is Latin for thousand.

CRM retargeting: A form of retargeting in which an e-mail address from a customer database is matched to web cookies. No personally identifiable information is passed.

data management platform (DMP): Technology platform that collects data from first- and third-party data sources and allows marketers to segment and act on that data.

dCPM: See dynamic CPM.

demand-side platform (DSP): Technology platform that manages multiple ad exchanges and data exchanges in one interface.

dynamic CPM: Auction-based pricing model in which the price per impression varies. Advertisers pay real market value for each individual ad impression and ensure price efficiency and transparency.

e-mail retargeting: A marketing technique that could either involve sending e-mails to people who complete a certain action (such as placing something in their shopping cart) or using activity within an e-mail (opening, clicking a link, and so on) as a trigger to either retarget or exclude a particular user from a campaign.

frequency cap: A limit of the number of times an ad can be shown to a particular user within a specified period.

IAB: Stands for Internet Advertising Bureau, an organization that is responsible for developing online advertising industry standards.

private exchange: An ad exchange controlled by a single entity usually consisting of premium, transparent inventory and where access is limited to select buyers.

real-time bidding (RTB): A system of buying and selling display advertising where an auction for a specific ad unit is held in real time as the page loads. Bidders must respond within an agreed-upon time limit (usually less than 50 milliseconds) with a bid amount and an ad they wish to show if they win the auction.

remnant (also known as remnant advertising): This refers to the ad impressions that are not sold through direct sales and are often sold at a large discount.

retargeting: See Chapters 1 to 14.

search retargeting: Targeting web users based on their prior search behavior.

site retargeting: Targeting web users based on their activity on a specific website.

supply-side platforms (SSP): A technology platform used by publishers to manage ad inventory and hooks into an ad exchange.

Index

Page references in *italics* refer to figures.